# Just Do The Damn Thing

How To Sit Your @ss Down
Long Enough
To Exert Willpower,
Develop Self Discipline,
Stop Procrastinating,
Increase Productivity,
And Get Sh!t Done

REESE OWEN

© Copyright 2018 by Reese Owen - All rights reserved.

The following eBook is reproduced below with the goal of providing information that is as accurate and reliable as possible. Regardless, purchasing this eBook can be seen as consent to the fact that both the publisher and the author of this book are in no way experts on the topics discussed within and that any recommendations or suggestions that are made herein are for entertainment purposes only. Professionals should be consulted as needed prior to undertaking any of the action endorsed herein.

This declaration is deemed fair and valid by both the American Bar Association and the Committee of Publishers Association and is legally binding throughout the United States.

Furthermore, the transmission, duplication or reproduction of any of the following work including specific information will be considered an illegal act irrespective of if it is done electronically or in print. This extends to creating a secondary or tertiary copy of the work or a recorded copy and is only allowed with express written consent from the Publisher. All additional rights reserved.

The information in the following pages is broadly considered to be a truthful and accurate account of facts, and as such any inattention, use or misuse of the information in question by the reader will render any resulting actions solely under their purview. There are no scenarios in which the publisher or the original author of this work can be in any fashion deemed liable for any hardship or damages that may befall them after undertaking information described herein.

Additionally, the information in the following pages is intended only for informational purposes and should thus be thought of as universal. As befitting its nature, it is presented without assurance regarding its prolonged validity or interim quality. Trademarks that are mentioned are done without written consent and can in no way be considered an endorsement from the trademark holder.

# ALL BOOKS BY REESE OWEN

Check out my other ebooks,
paperback books, and audiobooks:

### B*tch Don't Kill My Vibe
How To Stop Worrying, End Negative Thinking,
Cultivate Positive Thoughts,
And Start Living Your Best Life

### Just Do The Damn Thing
How To Sit Your @ss Down Long Enough To
Exert Willpower, Develop Self Discipline,
Stop Procrastinating, Increase Productivity,
And Get Sh!t Done

### Make Your Brain Your B*tch
Mental Toughness Secrets To Rewire Your Mindset
To Be Resilient And Relentless, Have Self Confidence
In Everything You Do,
And Become The Badass You Truly Are

REESE OWEN

# JUST DO THE DAMN THING

Since you're my friend—we're friends, right??—I'd like to give you my audiobook (~~usually $14.95~~) for **FREE**.

Search for my name
"Reese Owen" on Audible.

---

Audible member?  Use a credit.
New to Audible?  Get this audiobook **free** with your free trial.

# CONTENTS

**Introduction**     1

**Chapter 1: Sit Your Ass Down**     7

- ⇨ Get Real
- ⇨ Sometimes No Is Better Than Yes
- ⇨ The Right Kind Of Homies
- ⇨ How To Get A Toddler (Or A Low Functioning Adult) To Do Anything
- ⇨ It Begins At The Beginning
- ⇨ The Road To Hell Is Paved With Good Intentions
- ⇨ Breathe In. Hold It. Breathe Out.
- ⇨ Your Personal Bubble

**Chapter 2: If You Want It, Go Get It: Willpower for Beginners**     37

- ⇨ Sh*t Happens...And?
- ⇨ If You Mind, It Does Matter.
- ⇨ Powering Down In Three... Two... One...
- ⇨ Doing Things From Most Shitty To Least Sh*tty

**Chapter 3: The Dirty "S" Word**     53

- ⇨ Conquering Yourself
- ⇨ A Word To The Wise—Take The Words From The Wise
- ⇨ Create Your Habits Because Your Habits Are Creating You
- ⇨ The Devil On Your Shoulder
- ⇨ Who Has It, Who Doesn't, And Why It Doesn't Matter

## Chapter 4: Procrastination Nation — 73

- ⇨ It's Not Just You
- ⇨ Don't Live With It, Deal With It
- ⇨ Bite-Sized, Not Pint-Sized: How To Chew What You Are Biting Off
- ⇨ You're Never Going To Get There
- ⇨ You Are Amazing, Dammit

## Chapter 5: Effective Human Behavior — 95

- ⇨ Kiss Me, Fool
- ⇨ Who The Heck Is Ivy Lee?
- ⇨ Tomato Time
- ⇨ The Upside-Down
- ⇨ But What If I'm Not A Morning Person?
- ⇨ Tips For Getting Sh*t Done

## Chapter 6: **Get Ish Done** 131

⇨ One Thing At A Time, Bro
⇨ Permission To Be Pathetic

## Chapter 7: **Badass Blockers** 137

⇨ Badass, Or Just An Ass?
⇨ Smashing The Sh*t Out Of Your Goals

## Conclusion 143

# INTRODUCTION

We all know someone like Matt or Caroline.

Matt lives in his big house with a white picket fence and his two-car garage. He has a gorgeous wife and a baby Einstein for a child. His child has made the honor roll twice...at schools he's not even enrolled in. Their house is in a gated community and appears much too large for their three-person nuclear family. But, despite all appearances of success, Matt is not satisfied with his life. His job leaves him overworked and drained, having little time for his family, much less for any hobbies. He seems like he's got it all together on the outside, but every night, he drinks an entire bottle of wine while watching *The Real Housewives of Orange County* to numb himself from his misery.

He has always dreamed of starting up his own company. After all, he knows everything about cake pops and has a lot to offer. But, the prospect of leaving his current job and cushy salary is daunting. He loves that house that's way too big for him and his family. And if he's honest, he loves bragging about it even more—did he need the obnoxious two-story pergola in the front yard that was not approved by the HOA? Of course not. But he sounds good and feels important talking about it. He tells himself that he will take the plunge into the cake pop biz…one of these days. You can probably guess how many days ago that was.

And then there's Caroline. Caroline is a struggling college student—emphasis on the struggling. Like many students her age, she eats Ramen noodles for breakfast, lunch, and dinner—that's normal, right? All throughout high school, Caroline was able to balance school and a healthy social life, even if that did mean sacrificing a little bit of sleep. She worked hard to get into a good college so that she can work in her chosen field. But, it is a lot more difficult than she imagined.

She is now in debt over her head and is burnt out by constantly mindlessly ping-ponging back and forth between going to class that she's struggling in, studying material that she doesn't understand, writing papers that were due the week before, and trying to earn enough money at her part-time job to afford something other than freeze dried noodles for a meal.

One day, after getting only four hours of sleep, as Caroline is heading to class, she thinks...*Fiddlesticks*...as college life has gotten so hectic that she has had to cut back on shifts at her job, meaning she can no longer afford to buy a cup of coffee before class. Without the much needed caffeine boost, Caroline hopes that she can stay awake and listen to the professor. She can't risk going down another grade. Caroline knows that she could get more done if she cut back on some things and managed her time better, as that would enable her to book that tutor, get more sleep, cover more shifts at work, and eat less Ramen, but she doesn't know where to begin.

What do Matt and Caroline have in common? If you said they both have vowels in their names, you're wrong. Well, you're right, but that's not the point. Both Matt and Caroline struggle with procrastination, willpower, and the knowledge they need in order to get shit done. Therefore, their shit does not get done, and the quality of their lives suffers as a result. Are you like Matt or Caroline? Perhaps you too love cake pops, eat Ramen, and have an obnoxious oversized structure in your front yard.

There is no need to fear. With some knowledge and simple to implement tools, you will be able to stop procrastinating, find motivation, and get closer to achieving your goals. What are these tools? Well, I am so glad you asked because today, we are going to be talking about all of them. Perk up, grab a cup of black coffee (or a caffeinated sugary soda if you're soft), and get your pen and paper ready for notes. What we are about to talk about will change you so that you can change your life.

I know you have heard it all before. You've been told you need self-control. You need to be more motivated. You need to stop procrastinating. And you need more self-discipline, because without it, you will still procrastinate and be about as productive as an overfed house cat laying on a window sill. And of course, you've been told pretty much on a daily basis that you need to get your shit together. Blah blah blah.

Well, here you are. You obviously know you have a problem. You just don't know where to begin. And you're still at the same exact place you were when you wanted to make a change the last time around. Well, I am here to tell you that none of that matters now.

Get ready to dive deeper, change your thinking, and discover what it is that just didn't click into place for you before. All of the tools we'll discuss are interconnected. And they work. But if you don't implement them, then you can have all of the best intentions, yet never pass the finish line…or even the start line for that matter—yikes.

I want you to know that it's okay to be where you are. Truthfully, we have all been there. It's human nature to struggle with, well, our struggles. The thing that will set you apart from the person that didn't succeed is deciding not to let those struggles conquer you. While it's okay to be where you are, it's not okay to stay where you are when you know are capable of doing and being better.

Whether it's procrastination, a lack of productivity, or your ever-diminishing willpower, the following chapters will give you the insight you need to do those things you've been putting off that you know you should do, and live your life on purpose. You don't want to wake up one day only to realize the life you lived was an accidental train wreck of everything you believed to be out of your control. It *is* in your control.

While there may be *circumstances* in life out of your control, you *can* control how you react to them. Every moment is a by-product of the choices you make, and you can choose to make each moment better. Each following chapter, each section, each paragraph in this book will bring you closer to that truth and the life you desire. This is your life and you are the one behind the wheel. I believe in you. You got this, bro.

REESE OWEN

# CHAPTER 1:

## SIT YOUR ASS DOWN

It can be daunting to try to improve yourself, but you just have to begin at the beginning. Start by admitting your flaws, then make an effort to focus and buckle down so you can get things done. And that's what we'll cover in this chapter. Sure, it can be depressing admitting everything that's wrong with you, but you can only make the change you want in your life if you are honest with yourself, gather the tools you need (which you will find in this book), and make an earnest attempt to improve. But you have to do the work. There is no half-assing this, as that has never improved anything for anyone. Half-ass effort, half-ass life. And who wants half of an ass for a life?

## Get Real

This is the part where I grab you by the shoulders, stare into your eyes to the point where you're uncomfortable, then slap you. It's time to have *the talk*. You know the one. The talk about where you honestly stand right now.

Your mom lies to you about the time of Thanksgiving Dinner because she already knows that you will show up an hour and a half late. Have you seen that meme?: *Sorry I'm late, there was traffic and I left way after I told you.* Yeah, that was made for you. What's that in your bank account? Oh, nothing. A whopping $1.27. You don't bother opening the mail anymore because it's just another bill that you can't pay. Have you even checked your credit score? Yikes. I'd probably try to sweep that under the rug, too. When carpooling somewhere, your friends always offer to take their car, because they know when they open the door to yours, a combination of balled up receipts, dirty napkins, and french fry fossils will come avalanching out.

Any of this ring a bell? It's time to sit your ass down and start being honest with yourself about the issues you need to work on to get your ish together. It's time to stop digging yourself deeper into the hole that you are in because the further you dig, the harder it's going to be to climb out. You are not an ostrich, and burying your head in the sand is not going to help. Say it with me: *damage control.* You didn't say it. I said, say it with me. *Damage control.*

The first step to controlling the damage is deciding that you are ready for a change. A real change. For reals this time. Not like all of those other times you said you were ready, but then continued doing all the same crap that you have always done. After a certain point, it's not cute anymore.

Toddlers are cute when they flit around, going from one thing to another, never fully concentrating on or finishing anything, eating the cookie they weren't supposed to eat with their mouths and fingers covered in a combination of slobber and melted chocolate, avoiding the things they should do because they don't feel good. But once you're like, 30, it kind of loses its luster. You never complete anything. You have zero willpower or self-discipline. And you avoid doing anything that is remotely responsible.

And therefore, you can't seem to get ahead of where you are now. Promotions at work or graduating from grad school? Yeah, right. A nice place to live? Not if they lay eyeballs on that credit score. A car that doesn't make a shrieking bat sound every time you turn it on, leaving you praying that it won't completely disintegrate when you get it on the freeway? Not in the cards for you, buddy. Not at the rate you're going.

Let's check back in with Matt and Caroline to see how their lives are going.

Matt is tired. Tired of fighting, tired of always rushing, and tired of being tired. Once again, he was awake half of the night with insomnia, because after he got home from working, he and his wife got into another fight. It's his week to get the kid ready for school, but the next day, he has a rough time getting up after too little sleep, so rather than the quinoa avocado toast breakfast that his wife would prefer, he grabs the kid Twinkies on the way to school and hands him some money for lunch, entrusting him to make better food decisions than his dad did.

At his job, once again, Matt is in for yet another day of listening to a domineering boss with the IQ of a bag of Cheetos and the ego of Donald Trump. His boss doesn't even do anything at work—except make everyone around him miserable. Matt knows he is talented and does his job well, yet his boss does not appreciate his hard work.

Yet again, Matt zones out and begins daydreaming about cake pops, fantasizing about quitting his job and going out on his own. He thinks about starting to write a business plan…and then he stops thinking about it. As always, he pushes his idea of a cake pop fortune to the back burner. After work, it's time for bills, lawn mowing, taxes, and other miscellaneous adulting, and he is so worn out that he's unable to muster up the energy to do logic puzzles with his braniac kid. It's all simply work, dinner, wine, *Real Housewives of Orange County*, fight with wife, sleep, repeat.

And now let's check on Caroline.

Caroline's stomach was clenched in knots. In her fingers, she gripped her latest paper for one of her most important classes. She had dropped another grade, even though she bailed on some shifts at work to try to give herself extra time to study. Not only that, but her roommates have been on her case lately, saying she isn't pulling her share of the weight around the apartment, and they're fed up that she keeps paying her share of the bills late. She can see their point. Her room is a wreck, with piles of dirty laundry and about two weeks worth of dirty dishes that she never took to the kitchen. Her bedroom smells like a mixture of Hawaiian Breeze air freshener, mildew, and regret. Caroline doesn't get many visitors.

Worse yet, Caroline's boss just called and told her she was being let go. She had missed too many days of work and had been late too many times. They needed someone more reliable for the job. "*Dammit.*" she let out a long exhale and sat down on her unmade bed. Well, technically, she sat down on the pile of wrinkled laundry, dirty dishes, and empty styrofoam coffee cups on her unmade bed. Her car payment was now two months behind, and who could say when she would be able to pay it?

She put her head in her hands, and for the first time in a while, asked herself what in the freaking world was she doing with her life? How in the hell did she get herself into this shitty mess? More importantly, how was she going to get herself out of it?

Step One. Assess the damage. Truly assess the damage and see where you are currently. Don't be afraid to write down a list of all the things that are going terribly wrong in your life. Sometimes seeing it on paper can give you an extra nudge in the right direction. And taking inventory of where you are can make it more clear to you exactly where you need to go. There are plenty of people who have been where you are and plenty more who have been where Matt and Caroline are, too. The climb out is actually a pretty simple one. It seems overwhelming at first when you look at the big picture, but once you take that first step in the right direction, you will begin to realize how powerful you are and that nothing and no one can stand in your way unless you let them. If you just begin, you can be the badass you've always dreamed of being.

## Sometimes No Is Better Than Yes

"*Hey, wanna go out again tonight?*" You really should tell them no because you have a presentation first thing in the morning at work tomorrow. Yet, here you are, after a pathetic excuse for an internal struggle (you basically just immediately said yes), climbing into your friend's car and going out for drinks. Again. For the third time this week. And it's Wednesday.

We all have at least one friend that talks us into ignoring our responsibilities. After all, it's an easy and comfortable thing to do when they are ignoring their responsibilities, too. That little voice in the back of your mind telling you that you've got more important things to do is squashed out by your friend telling you that you'll be fine and it really isn't that big of a deal. You begin to make excuses to yourself, even though you only half believe them. "*I deserve a break, just for one night,*" "*I can catch up on the work tomorrow,*" "*It's just this one time.*"

This isn't me telling you that having a night out with friends is a bad thing. This isn't even me trying to say that your friend is a bad friend. This is me telling you that you need to learn to say no and that your priorities are askew. That's right—askew. We have twenty-four hours in a day and what you do with the time you're given matters.

What you spend your time on shows in your life. You can look at someone's life, and immediately tell how they're spending their time. If you spend your time getting distracted, that is going to reflect in your professional or academic performance. Which is totally fine, you know, if you want to stay in the same exact place you are right now instead of moving forward. Maybe you like the bat shrieking car.

But if you don't, you need to be aware of the people in your life. If you have someone who is constantly dragging you down and holding you back, then have a talk with them. Tell them what you need to see changed. Either they'll understand and back off with the incessant body-shots-and-dancing-on-tables invitations, or they won't get it and you'll have to ask yourself if it's worth having their influence in your life any longer. You deserve to have friends who support you and your endeavors. This may mean that for some of your friends, you can't hang out with them as much…or ever.

This is especially true if your friend is a toxic one. If you find that your friend is unsupportive, manipulative, perpetually negative, or taking out their repressed emotions on you and others, then they are draining you of your emotional energy. These toxic people—we'll call them vampires—not only take away your emotional energy, but they can also increase your anxiety. In extreme cases, they can even contribute to feelings of depression.

If you find that one of your "friends" sucks in the way that we just described, and rather than enjoying spending time with them you end up dreading it, then spend time examining the true heart of your friendship. Better yet, skip the examination, and just give them the boot. Maybe your time will be better spent examining why you allowed such a toxic person to remain in your life as long as you did.

The company you keep will keep you. So ask yourself: where do you want to be kept? Is it where you are at now or do you really want to make a change? Think about that the next time you want to skip something important because an invitation from a loser came up.

## The Right Kind Of Homies

I may have been a little harsh in that last section. I don't mean to imply that all your friends are losers. While you may have some toxic vampires in your life, you might just have some great friends that genuinely care about you. In order to reach your goals, you don't necessarily need to wave your hand in the air with a "*later, bitches!*" to *all* your friends.

You need a support system around you of ambitious, go-getting, doers. Good friends are more than willing to help the people they care about reach their goals because they want to ride your coattails and be in your entourage when you make it. Just kidding. They want to see you succeed as much as you want to yourself. Spend more time with these friends. Talk to them. Tell them your goals and the steps you plan to take to reach them. This includes telling them about how you need to lessen distractions and stop procrastinating. They can help hold you accountable.

Even though they may be good peeps though, for the sake of making sure you have enough time to achieve your goals, you may still need to cut back on time hanging out with them. Your thrice a week game night may have to go down to once. You can also find other ways to spend time together that will be productive for both of you.

Trade in a night riding mechanical bulls at Saddle Ranch for a coffee shop work day. Or, run your weekly errands together. An oil change, grocery shopping trip, or car wash is much more fun with a buddy. What you need to be sure of is that the time you spend with your friends isn't causing long-term negative consequences. If you like to drink and party, keep in mind that a night of drinking isn't likely to promote either a healthy body, healthy bank account, or wise choices. Sometimes, it's good to say no the party and yes to productivity.

## How To Get A Toddler (Or A Low Functioning Adult) To Do Anything

I know you've been there. You're ready this time. Like, *really* ready. You've finally psyched yourself into sitting down at your desk and getting started on typing that project. You said an hour of affirmations. You wrote out a game plan. You spent a day and a half cleaning your workspace so you could get ready for this moment. You crack your knuckles. Your fingers approach your computer keyboard triumphantly. *Eye of the Tiger* starts playing in your head. And then it happens. The notifications and the distractions start rolling in...

*Melissa just posted on her Facebook page that she and her husband had a baby. Hm. I didn't even know she was married.*

*Oh—Beth just texted me—Melissa got married.*

*An email just came in: Three people viewed my LinkedIn profile today. I have been looking for a new job. Maybe I should check my LinkedIn right now.*

*Oh, wow, that hot guy finally responded to me on Bumble. I should definitely respond to him right now. A guy who mentors inner city kids, loves his mother, and can wiggle his ears is hard to find. I can do my project later. I don't want to die single.*

*I'm actually getting hungry. And there's a new episode of Grey's Anatomy on Hulu. Maybe I should eat and watch Grey's Anatomy. I can think better on a full stomach. And maybe Grey's Anatomy will inspire me with ideas for this project I have to do that has absolutely nothing to do with Grey's Anatomy.*

*I need a break. I know I haven't started yet, but…I need a break.*

We all have a million and one different things pulling us in a million different directions, none of which lead to the accomplishment of our goals. Know the distractions in your life. Our phones and social media seem to be the biggest instigators nowadays. It's all too easy to pick up your phone "just for a second," "just to check real quick," and before you know it, you've wasted hours of your day and have made zero progress on your project, but you did manage to catch up on an entire season of *Grey's Anatomy*, find out everything about your ex-boyfriend's new girlfriend, update your Tinder profile, and order an Asian Man Peel and Stick Wall Decal on Amazon. It's really a thing, look it up.

However, this is where I want to challenge yourself. I want you to put an end to frolicking in the realm of distractions and start seeing them for what they are—obstacles. Beautiful, fun, comfy, shiny, instant gratification obstacles that you allow to impede your own path and keep you from doing the things you want and need to get done.

I don't know if you have ever dealt with a child, but one thing that I have noticed about children is that positive reinforcement is the way to go. This system also works with pets in case you were wondering. (I mean, kids and pets are basically the same thing, right?)

Now, when you ask a little kid to do something, their knee-jerk reaction is usually to not do it, because, at the end of the day, we all really want to know what's in it for us. If we are going to be going out of our way to do something, we don't want to waste our time doing something that is neither fun nor helpful to us in some way. So what works? How do you get a kid to do something you want them to do? Bribery. You're welcome for the free parenting advice.

When little Jimmy won't pick up his toys and clean his room, you tell him he'll get an ice cream sandwich when he's done, and before you can even get to the end of your sentence, his room is spic and span. You need to parent yourself as if you are an obnoxious spoiled child that only responds to promises of ice cream.

Next time you want to flop on the couch and binge watch everything on Netflix and Hulu, do this instead: tackle at least one thing on your *I've been meaning to do that* list and then reward yourself with a not-so-productive distraction. No cheating though. You can't do five minutes of work and reward yourself with five hours of television. If you know you really need to read a book to prepare for a project, then tell yourself that you can watch one episode of TV after you've read the first half of the book. Do what makes sense. Not what makes sense to the part of your that can't get your shit together, but do what makes sense to the part of you that shakes its finger in judgment at the part of you that can't get your shit together.

Dr. Bill Knaus, licensed clinical psychologist and former psychology professor, has studied extensively on the subject of procrastination. He has discovered what he refers to as "paradoxical procrastination rewards." These involve giving in to those unplanned, unstructured distractions that we talked about earlier. The "quick" coffee break from the work you haven't even started yet, the "quick" response to the text message that just popped up on your phone, the "quick" Facebook status update you post about how you're feeling distracted and can't seem to get any work done—things like this may make you feel better in the short-term since they are taking away whatever incomplete task stressed you out, thereby temporarily eliminating the source of your stress, anxiety, and discomfort.

But in the long-term, they are actually getting in the way of your goals by making you more likely to procrastinate. How does that happen? These false rewards become habits in your brain. They reinforce your impulsive nature, thus solidifying your weakened willpower. Soon, without even giving it any thought, you will find yourself procrastinating because your brain knows it feels good. Paradoxical procrastination rewards are a perfect illustration of the saying, "pain of discipline vs pain of regret."

It doesn't always feel good to do the responsible thing. The short term satisfaction of giving in to distraction feels good in the moment when you are ignoring your responsibility, but then down the road, when you look up and realize you're financially and emotionally bankrupt, living in your parents' basement, and never made anything of yourself, you don't feel so good.

The good news is, there is hope. Dr. Knaus has also found that procrastination reversal methods are an effective means not only to be productive but to get your brain back out of the sinking pit of the procrastination habit. When you tell yourself you will accomplish a set amount of work, or work for a specific time period before rewarding yourself, and stick to this, then after a period of two weeks, you will find that you are much less likely to even consider procrastinating. It's all about establishing the habit of productivity for the habit of procrastination. Oh, and bribery. Don't forget bribery.

Over time, as you being to see the fruits of your labor, you'll find yourself enjoying the more long-term rewards of getting things done over the short term rewards that go along with pushing things off. Some of the benefits of these procrastination reversal rewards that Dr. Knaus mentions are:

1. You prove to yourself (and to your nosy, overly judgmental loved ones) that you can in fact control your impulses. This is not only a boost in confidence, but it can also lessen stress.

2. You learn to enjoy constructive rewards rather than destructive "rewards." And the satisfaction of earning a constructive reward feels even stronger when you've successfully fought the impulse of giving in to the destructive reward. Not to mention, you get to avoid the guilt that often quickly follows giving in to destructive rewards.

3. By teaching yourself to get out of the vicious cycle of procrastination, you can more easily organize your day, get things done with less time and energy, lessen distractions, and of course increase productivity.

## It Begins At The Beginning

It starts first thing in the morning when you roll out of bed and slap your alarm clock until it stops making that obnoxious noise in your face…you know, the noise that you told it to make when you set it last night an extra hour earlier than usual, telling yourself triumphantly *"tomorrow is going to be the day!"* And now that tomorrow is here, as soon as your alarm goes off, how are you starting your day? Your attitude.

Your attitude and what you tell yourself in that one moment is already steering your day in the direction you are going to go. What kind of things are you telling yourself? Are you already thinking, *"Damn, all of this shit again? I'm exhausted. I'm not doing it again today. I can't wait to go back to bed. I'll be glad when this is over with."* Well, then, why not just go back to bed? No really, I mean it. If you are waking up and you have already let yourself be defeated, then you are just wasting your time and your day isn't going to look any different than the day before it. In fact, your stress levels will only go up, making your day even worse. So, you might as well just live your life in bed, grumbling at the world, complaining about how your life sucks and you're not doing anything about it.

Or, I have a better idea. Rise up to the challenge of the day. When you wake up, decide that you can handle everything life throws at you. Because you can. There isn't a single day that you have lived that you haven't gotten through. Granted, some of those days may have been harder than others, but you've still made it through. And that starts with one thing: deciding you can.

Set some time aside to consider your day. You have a brain, use it. Take some time when you are starting out your day to think about what that day needs to look like. Ask yourself, *what are the three most important things I can do today to move my life forward in the direction that I want it to go?* I don't care if it's ten minutes in your car in the freaking Starbucks drive through, or even a couple minutes when you're in the shower. Take a few minutes at the beginning of each day to ask yourself this critical question so you can start making your days happen instead of letting your days happen to you.

Now, you also have to remember that if you start your day off right, you have to make sure that things or people outside of you don't throw you off. We all have those days that we start out on the right path and then comes the asshole with the huge unnecessarily loud truck, and the tiny….well…something else. He cuts you off and makes you hit the red light when you're already running late. How dare he? He *knew* you left the house too late and were already late for work, and he shouldn't have gotten in front of you. Sitting with this thought leaves you pissed at him…all day. You would have been more productive today if that douchebag wouldn't have cut you off. Right? It's his fault you can't get your life together.

Now, come on. Don't let a douchebag with a small member ruin your day and derail your life. Don't sweat it. Douchebags happen. You need to be prepared for these shitty moments so you can protect your day and protect your time.

You need an *"in case of emergency, break glass"* plan to help you reset when needed. Personally, I like using a phrase. It can be whatever you want it to be. Mine is *"You're not crazy, you're in control. You are not crazy. You. Are. In. Control."* Words from the movie *31* and the wise and articulate Rob Zombie. Sure, the guy in the movie may have been a few fries short of a Happy Meal, but that doesn't mean we can't learn something from him. I mean, he was very successful at what he did, so there is something to be said for that.

No matter what the hell falls into your lap during your day, you decide how to react and you decide what comes after.

## The Road To Hell Is Paved With Good Intentions

What if your life sucks, and you really are trying? Like, really. This isn't your first rodeo trying to get a grip. Maybe you've been making to-do lists, writing down your goals, and chasing after them like a golden retriever after a worn-out tennis ball. Well, I'm here to tell you that not trying hard enough isn't the only thing that can get between you and your goals. Trying too hard can be just as bad, and can be a contributing factor to a major problem.

What is this major problem? *Burnout.*

Burnout is especially prevalent in two types of people. Firstly, those in the common "helping" job fields such as doctors, nurses, and psychologists. Not only do these jobs often have long hours, but they take a toll physically and mentally, as well.

Secondly, high achievers. Are you someone who used to be a go-getter, a type A person, someone who was always accomplishing something? Only to then find yourself slowly losing energy until you found yourself losing your motivation and developing habits of procrastination? Before you even realized it, you may have begun to feel like you lost yourself, and like you don't know who you are anymore.

Taking on an extremely high workload can be both physically and mentally draining. And expecting too much of yourself and putting too many to do's on your plate are also physically and mentally draining, and not conducive to getting anything done. The human body isn't meant to run twenty-four/seven, yet in today's society, people are praised for coming to work early, and staying late, day in and day out, stacking up vacation days and personal days that they'll never use.

Not only does burnout reduce your productivity and energy, but it also raises your anxiety, increases your risk of depression, makes you more cynical, leaves you feeling helpless, and before long, you may become downright resentful and turn into that grumpy old man that's always telling people to get off his lawn and whose life advice consists of telling everyone life sucks so don't bother trying. If you keep pushing yourself, eventually, you will simply have nothing more to give. You won't give a damn if it all goes to hell. You let the shit hit the fan, because you are simply out of anything left to give.

The effects of burnout are profound, as it can affect every aspect of your life. You will find not only does your work life suffer, but your home and social life do, as well. Even your health will suffer. The long-term exhaustion and stress will leave you more vulnerable to catching colds, the flu, or even having a heart attack. If you believe you may be experiencing job burnout, don't ignore it. Prioritize your health, make time for periods of rest, and if it gets serious, talk to your doctor. Don't go *karoshi* on me. The Japanese actually have a word for sudden occupational death—karoshi. Don't let that be you.

To start, here are a few tips well-known to help aid in treating work-related burnout, that even have the *Harvard Business Review* seal of approval:

- **Prioritize Your Self-Care**

    Make time to take care of both your physical and mental health. This means giving yourself a proper night's sleep, eating well, exercising, engaging with friends, and maybe even meditating. If you have a difficult time fitting these things into your schedule, write down everything you spend your time on for a week. You can log this on your phone, or an analog piece of paper, whichever your preference.

Don't just track time spent on each activity, but for each activity, take note of how much of a toll it takes on you or how much it energizes you. Rank everything on a scale of 1-10, using 0 for *I feel like I just got run over by an 18-wheeler* and 10 for *I want to run up a mountain and spin around in circles joyously, arms outstretched like in the Sound of Music*.

After the week is over, not only will you be provided a detailed look into how you spend your time and where you can improve, but it can help you decide what may be taking more of a toll on your health than it is worth. You may simply need to be more intentional about your time, using it in a way that will promote your emotional and physical well-being rather than mindlessly watching TV all night after spending all day at a job that makes you want to stick needles in your eyes.

- **Change Things Up**

If your job is draining, there are many ways in which you can shift your perspective in order to help prevent mental burnout. Obviously, you can try to be more positive and less cynical, but this alone does not usually help in the long run. Along with trying to have a more positive mindset, try to make changes around the office or workspace that can lessen stress.

If you feel underappreciated, you can try to showcase just how much value you provide the company. A little peacocking never hurt anybody. If you have coworkers who are loud or obnoxious, try to foster a good work relationship with the ones you get along with better, to counterbalance the negative coworkers. If you have too much on your plate, see if you can delegate any of your workload among those who are lazy aren't as busy.

- **Speak Up**

You may need to put your foot down in the workplace and at home, letting co-workers, your boss, and friends and loved ones know that you are trying to make changes that improve your health and your productivity levels. Let them know that there is a limit of what you can take on. If your boss is wanting you to come in early and leave late without extra pay, there's a diplomatic, professional way to have a conversation with them about how you can't do that. If your friends are expecting you to constantly go out every day after work, let them know that while you still love to hang out with them, you need opportunities to recuperate.

- **Cultivate Connections**

Yes, we have said repeatedly that you can't just go out partying with friends every night. Although, that does not mean you don't need to build bonds with other people. Friendships and relationships are important. Humans are not meant to live just to work. While you need to set boundaries with your loved ones if they are pushing you to spend excessive amounts of time with them to the point of your own exhaustion, it is still important to spend time with those whom you care about.

When we are spending all of our time on work and trying to get ahead, we gradually become more stressed, anxious, depressed, and cynical. Spending time with friends can rejuvenate us, and remind us of what is important in life. Even if you can't get together in-person to hang out with a friend, remember that you live in the $21^{st}$ century, and you can call, text, Facebook message, Facetime, Skype…I mean, the list goes on and on.

- **You Don't Have To Stay**

While finding a new job is easier said than done, you may need to consider it. If you find your job is constantly draining you for one reason or another, and you are stressed just thinking about going into work, you may need to take the plunge, and find another job in your field, or even an entirely different field. Reducing your stress levels and your *I hate my life, kill me now* levels will truly benefit your long-term health and goals.

Before thinking of a list of reasons why you can't leave your job, take a minute and write down a list of why you can—or better yet, why you must. Then, after you see why you can and why you should, make a plan on *how* you can. Remember, think the long view. How can you help yourself get into a different occupational situation that will get you closer to your long-term goals and where you ultimately want to be in your life?

## Breathe In. Hold It. Breathe Out.

At the risk of sounding like a hippy in the forest, *Take a deep breath in. And hold it. Count one, two, three, four, and five. Now breathe it all out.*

If you are thinking breathing shouldn't be considered as a tool for you to use to gain back control of your life since you've been doing it all your life, then consider this. If a pregnant woman in unimaginable, mind-numbing, body breaking, indescribable amounts of pain can use breathing to help her through giving birth, then you can use breathing to help you clear your mind.

Breathing sounds very basic but all of the stuff you are tripping over in your head can be calmed down with the use of deep and slow breathing.

What happens when we breathe? I mean, really breathe. According to *The American Institute of Stress* and Dr. Herbert Benson, deep breathing creates a relaxation response, which will then change the way our bodies and minds react to stress. Some of the physiological reactions to the relaxation response include:

- Decreased Heart Rate
- Relaxed Muscle Tension
- Lower Blood Pressure
- Naturally Slowed Breathing
- Increased Nitric Oxide Levels
- Decreased Metabolism

Now, laying on the couch doing nothing does not activate this relaxation response, but rather, it is activated when you are mentally active, calm, focused, and breathing deeply. In fact, *The American Institute of Stress* found that twenty to thirty minutes of deep abdominal breathing a day can greatly reduce stress and anxiety. This process will increase the amount of oxygen in your brain, which stimulates the parasympathetic portion of your nervous system, helping to physically minimize stress. Ooh, I sound smart, don't I?

These are real changes happening in your body that help you when you are stressed out. There is a reason therapists use breathing techniques to help their clients cope with stress.

When you use controlled breathing, you take back that control over yourself that only you have and you are able to slow it down and focus on handling what is right in front of you. The best part? You can do it anywhere at any time and you don't even have to pay for a doctor to do it, which is especially exciting if you live in the US, given the cost of healthcare. They say an apple a day keeps the doctor away. Well, deep breathing is the new apple.

## Your Personal Bubble

Now that you are feeling nice and relaxed, it's time to discover how to keep it that way. It's important to have a bubble. A bubble is a place that is yours and yours alone. No one can come into your bubble unless you invite them in. It's like when you were a kid and you made a secret clubhouse.

Creating this bubble around yourself is important. You need this space to recharge from daily life and the things that drain you until you've been worn out as thin as that t-shirt you've had since seventh grade that your mom's been begging you to throw away.

If you find yourself feeling depleted, like you are constantly giving away yourself to everyone and everything else in your life, then think about the last time you really had time for yourself. The last time you were able to do the things that recharge and energize you. If it's been a while, perhaps you haven't created a bubble or maintained it very well.

Think of your cell phone. It has the capability to do everything from the smallest to the largest of tasks. However, as neat and useful as our phones are, they are useless if you don't put them on the charger. A dead battery won't get you anything. They need to be recharged often in order for you to be able to get any use out of them. You, my friend, are like a cell phone.

Think about somewhere you can go where you can relax away from the constant onslaught of the world around you. If you don't have a place in mind already, create one. And as important as it is to have a relaxation bubble, it's also good to have a productivity bubble.

Have a dedicated, sacred space that you can work in to work towards your goals. A home office, a corner of your bedroom, the dining room table after dinner time, any place you can dedicate as your own space, even temporarily, where everyone you live with knows not to bother you while you're working there. This is the place where you can have uninterrupted time to write the book, build the website, start that side hustle, whatever happens to be on your list.

REESE OWEN

# CHAPTER 2:

## IF YOU WANT IT, GO GET IT: WILLPOWER FOR BEGINNERS

Is life throwing challenges at you like those really annoying boys from middle school P.E. who just wouldn't let up during dodgeball? And do you find yourself continuing to get hit like those poor little scrawny girls with taped together glasses who look like they've never touched a single piece of athletic equipment in their lives? When life keeps throwing things at you, it's easy to want to curl up in fetal position and avoid the things we know we need to get done. But do you want to know how to beat the procrastination monster and get ish done? It all starts with finding your willpower. In this chapter, we will explore how to find *and keep* your willpower.

## Shit Happens…And?

You spilled your latte. The hot water tank burst and you had to take a cold shower. You ran over a nail on the way to work and are now running late again. I get it. Yes, shit happens, but, it's time to stop letting situational excuses control your life. Successful people don't live lives where nothing bad ever happens to them. They just choose to overcome it and work past it anyway to get to where they are going without using their situations as an excuse for why they didn't do what they needed to do. And here you are, saying *I don't feel like it* or *I don't want to anymore* because something happened that wasn't perfect.

Your life is not going to be perfect, and no one is going to fix your life for you. So stop using the imperfection of your life as a reason to put things off and not work to get things done. In fact, you should be using the imperfection of your life as a reason to motivate you to get things done. Every single person you encounter in your day-to-day life is putting out their own fires. They are battling their own demons and their own issues. The weight of your life is on your shoulders, and you are the only person in this world that can handle it. It's on you. We can be our own worst, self-sabotaging enemy or we can be our own best friend and biggest cheerleader. At the end of the day, which do you think is going to give you a better life?

If you're one of those workout types, you know that muscle is built by repeatedly lifting things too heavy for you, the strain of which causes muscle tissue to break down. While it may be difficult at first, as your body adjusts, it will not only heal, but strengthen. Before you know it, the weights you were struggling with will now seem light.

When you feel like there is too much on your shoulders, stand up straight and lift your chin. Remember that you will survive, you will get through whatever life throws at you. You have gotten through all of your worst days until now, and you can continue to overcome them. When the world crumbles around you, have a look at the wreckage and build a new life out of all the pieces that are still there. When you spill coffee on your favorite pants, get new pants! These are not excuses to stop you. Remember, you are still here. The heartbeat of most humans is around four thousand beats per hour. Each pulse, each throb, is a trophy with the words *I'm still freaking here!* engraved on it. You are winning four thousand trophies an hour. You are a winner. You are still alive and should act like it.

I think I'm going to need some of that deep breathing from the last chapter to recover from that very cinematic and theatrical rant, but the point is—when something happens unexpectedly that derails you on the way to achieving your goal, remind yourself that hey, shit happens, and you're going to forge ahead anyway. Where there's a will, there's a way.

**If You Mind, It Does Matter.**

*I think, therefore, I am.*

We can all agree that there is a vast difference in our bodies when we eat healthy versus when we eat shit. Or if we fill up with water or fill up with some questionable liquid with 48 grams of sugar and yellow #5.

If what we fuel our bodies with can profoundly affect our bodies, then why wouldn't what we fuel our minds with profoundly affect our minds?

The famous actor, Jim Carrey, has provided inspiring messages in which he shares with us some insight on the effects of positive thinking when paired with visualization. In one of these messages, he discusses how when he was completely broke and penniless that he would visualize opportunities coming to him. He would accept that while he did not yet possess these things, he would someday. The opportunities were out there and waiting for him.

To keep himself inspired, Jim wrote himself a check for ten million dollars, and placed it in his wallet as a constant reminder. He believed that no matter how long it took, he would achieve this goal. When writing the check, he dated it for Thanksgiving of 1995, and even though that check slowly deteriorated, he saved it. Sure enough, shortly before Thanksgiving of the year that he had dated the check for, he learned that he would earn those ten million dollars on his movie *Dumb and Dumber*.

Now, is Jim Carrey a witch or some sorcerer genie with magical powers? No. What he did stems from psychology and illustrates the power and veracity of the idea that we can manifest and attract what we hold in our minds. He believed that he could, which made him open to all of life's opportunities. He didn't let negative thoughts such as *"I'm never going to make it"* or *"I can't do that"* or *"That might happen for someone else but not for me"* control his effort and will and act as a barricade between where he was and where he wanted to be.

Visualization and deliberately choosing to hold on to positive, optimistic thoughts only works if you put in the effort and hard work. If you make some half-ass attempt to visualize your success and tell yourself once or twice *"I think I can, I think I can,"* and then forget about it and never put the true effort in, then you will not see the benefits of this practice.

What we tell ourselves about ourselves impacts us on a greater scale than we even realize. Think about the types of people that you see that are extremely successful in their daily lives. They hold confidence and self-assurance. They possess tenacity and resilience. More often than not, they didn't even start out any different than you or me. They simply fought for what they believed in, which was themselves.

In a very interesting TED Talk, *How to Make Stress Your Friend*, psychologist Kelly McGonial dives into a very interesting theory that goes against what a lot of us have trained ourselves to believe about stress. In this concept, she captures just what happens when we change the way that we think about something and the way that it biologically impacts our bodies.

She started out by confessing that for the past ten years, she has been teaching people that stress is harmful, that it makes you sick and increases your chance of death. Stress is the Regina George of your life. *Mean Girls*, anyone? Basically, stress is the enemy. Yet, she has now changed her mind about stress, and she wants to change the mind of everyone else as well.

She goes on to tell us about a study that made her rethink her entire approach to stress. This study tracked 30,000 adults in the United States for eight years and they started this study by asking, "How much stress have you experienced in the last year?" They followed that question with "Do you believe that stress is harmful to your health?" They then used public death records to figure out who died.

She tells us the bad news first. People who had experienced a lot of stress in the previous year had a 43% increased chance of dying but that was only true for the people who believed that stress was bad for your health. People who experienced a lot of stress, but did not view stress as harmful for their health, were no more likely to die. In fact, they had the lowest risk of dying than anyone else in the study, including people who experience relatively little stress.

She expands on this idea by telling us of another study that was conducted at Harvard University where participants were given a social stress test. This stress test was designed to stress you the hell out. Kind of like the shopping experience in the labyrinth of a place they call IKEA.

The participants in this study were informed prior to taking the test to reconsider their stress, and to think of it as a healthy and helpful response. They were encouraged to think that the pounding in your heart prepares you to take action, and breathing more quickly increases oxygen in your brain. You know what happened? The participants who learned this method, and reconsidered stress as helpful felt overall less stressed afterward. These people became more confident and less anxious.

In a typical stress response, the heart rate will increase and blood vessels will constrict. This is one of the main reasons why stress can cause cardiovascular diseases. This is not a healthy state to be at consistently. Yet, the study found that in the participants who viewed their stress as something helpful, their blood vessels did not constrict.

The heart rate was still elevated, but the lack of constriction of their blood vessels caused them to fit a much more healthy profile for cardiovascular health. This response was actually similar to what can happen to your cardiovascular system when you are experiencing joy or courage. How you think about stress and how you manage it matters. Or, more simply, how you think matters.

Now, what is the line of comparison that we can draw from Jim Carrey, a very famous, non-wizard comedic actor, and Kelly McGonial, a health psychologist? Hint, I kind of just said it. It's that what we think and what we tell ourselves has an impact on our lives. If you tell yourself that you are never going to get out of this rut and that your life will never change, and you believe it, then you are right. However, if you tell yourself that this is only one more hurdle that you have to jump over, but that you can and will overcome it, then you are right.

Our minds are very powerful, which means each and every one of us has the capacity to be very powerful. It doesn't matter if the person next to you started out ahead of you with more money and more advantages. It's what you tell yourself that will determine how far *you* can go. What you tell yourself will factor into where you inevitably end up. So, think about it, are you telling yourself that you aren't capable of something? Because you are. It all begins with that voice inside your head.

## Powering Down In Three… Two… One…

The American Psychological Association explains a theory known as "willpower depletion." This theory states that in one form or another, you have to exert a certain amount of willpower every day. Whether you are choosing to write your business plan and resist the urge to pick up your phone, or reaching for a healthy dinner rather than picking up fast food, or even choosing to keep your mouth shut rather than saying something snide to someone you think deserves your wrath—studies have shown that after consistently resisting temptations, it begins to take a mental toll and our willpower is like a muscle which can become fatigued with overuse.

Some early evidence supporting this theory came from the lab of Dr. Roy Baumeister. In one of his studies, he had some of his participants sit in a room with freshly-baked cookies and a bowl of radishes. Some of these participants were asked to taste the cookies, while others the radishes. Afterward, the participants were asked to complete a difficult geometric puzzle in the span of thirty minutes.

Dr. Baumeister found that those who ate the radishes and resisted the cookies gave up on the puzzle after eight minutes, on average. Whereas, the people who were able to enjoy the cookies spent nineteen minutes, on average, attempting the puzzle. The people who ate the radishes and, therefore, had to exert willpower to avoid the cookies, were more drained of motivation and self-control when it came to the puzzle.

The American Psychological Association goes on to tell us that when we are dealing with hostile people, whether co-workers or in-laws, we may feel emotionally and physically exhausted. But, this type of exhaustion is different from simple sleepiness as a result of sleep deprivation. Dr. Vohs conducted a study on twenty-four hours of sleep deprivation on participants and then asked them to suppress their emotions in response to a film clip. Dr. Vohs then tested the emotional self-control of the participants, and to her surprise, she found that the participants who had been sleep deprived were no more likely to be depleted of willpower than people who had slept soundly.

That raises the question, if willpower depletion isn't a type of physical fatigue, then what actually is it? Recent studies have shown that a possible mechanism that affects human willpower and its depletion could include functions at the biological level. The University of Toronto has found that those who had their willpower depleted by tasks that require self-control also had a decrease of activity in the anterior cingulate cortex of the brain, which is an important region for cognition. This shows that when our willpower has been pushed, our brains may actually function at a lesser degree.

What does any of this mean for us? They've been lying to us all along and we should skip the veggies and gorge on cookies? Not quite.

Like any other muscle, if you overexert it, then you will experience a negative impact on your body and a diminished ability (at least temporarily) to properly use that muscle. Imagine trying to drive a car without gas in the tank. Doesn't work. You wouldn't just expect your car to get your where you need to be with an empty tank, would you? You would put gas in the car so it can help you get to your destination. Well, willpower is essentially the fuel that drives you. So fuel that bad boy up, decide where you need to go, make sure you don't run out of gas on your way, and get there.

Practice using your self-control and willpower frequently, and before long, you will find the tasks that used to be hard to use willpower to accomplish will become easier. The driving force behind us going after the things in life that we want is willpower. A common misconception is that some people just have more willpower than others. Like any other muscle in your body, if you don't use it, then you lose it. If willpower is like a muscle, then we all have it. Some people just seem like they have more because they've been working out their willpower longer than others.

## Doing Things From Most Shitty To Least Shitty

The most simple and straightforward tip for most effectively managing your willpower and beating procrastination into the ground is to prioritize completing the most important item on your to-do list each day. The most important thing is also often the most difficult thing. But it's the task that will move the needle so to speak, the task that will get you closest to the accomplishment of your goal. So before you wash the dishes, vacuum, or shop online for that new air fryer, first work on that important grant proposal that you are putting off. While this may sound like a simple concept, aside from successful entrepreneurs, most people don't do this.

People often feel most productive when they are getting a bunch of things done during the day, but in actuality, crossing off a million to do's each day can reduce your productivity. Why? Because when you are "accomplishing" items of mild importance one after another, then you aren't going to get to what is actually most important because your willpower tank and your time will be depleted before you get to it.

Think *what can I do that will help me reach my biggest goals?*

Let's revisit our old friend Caroline, who you met earlier. She is overwhelmed by the thought of an essay that she has due. Because that's how it always works, doesn't it? We're overwhelmed by the *thought* of doing a thing more so than the actual *doing* of the thing.

So, Caroline has this big essay due. But, she also has a long to-do list. Rather than getting started on the essay right away, she decides to tackle her Mt. Everest-sized laundry pile first. She tells herself that while she cleans, she can think through what she needs to write. Then she decides to go to the store and get an air freshener in an attempt to make her room smell like something that doesn't singe your nose hairs. After all, getting out of the house will give her a moment to refresh her mind. But she can't just get any old air freshener. She has to pick the perfect scent, so she ends up being one of those people who sprays every single fragrance, making anyone who walks down the aisle cough up a lung.

When Caroline gets back to her place, she decides to tackle those dishes that are starting to grow fungus. Then she moves to organizing her mail piles—*overdue bills*, and *super duper overdue bills*. Caroline has allowed herself to get repeatedly distracted, pushing off her most important task of the day. By the time Caroline is done with her cleaning, she has some happy roommates, yes, but she is worn out and is only able to write half a paragraph of her essay, and what she does write is only C+ level at best.

Many of us try to squeeze in as many menial tasks as possible each day as if it's the last day we have on earth to tie up our loose ends. Rather than doing this just to feel productive, actually *be* productive and focus on what is actually important to you and your goals, first. Yes, the dishes may need to be washed, but if you need to write that essay more, begin with that essay first. The dishes can always come later.

If you always start the day with accomplishing the item with the most importance, you can ensure that you get it done, that nothing comes up to prevent you from accomplishing it, and that you don't wear yourself out before you get the chance to do what really matters.

You'll find that this is very helpful for your willpower. The biggest item takes the most willpower, therefore, if you wait until late in the day to accomplish it, you might have depleted your willpower tank, making it hard to accomplish anything. You will have the most willpower at the beginning of the day when you have not yet had to use it for more than getting out of bed. And for some of us, even that can use a lot of willpower, so you'd definitely better get started on your biggest tasks first, because by the time you brush your teeth in the morning, you could already be working with a low tank.

Consider this, all of your most important and tedious tasks are like weights. Each one weighs you down more and more the more you put things off until you feel like it's going to be impossible to reach your goals, be the best version of yourself, or simply just get anything done. The second you take that heaviest weight off of your shoulders, everything else on your plate is going to feel a whole lot lighter, spiraling you into something I like to call momentum. I said that as if I made up the word momentum.

You probably know what momentum is, but for the sake of clarity, Merriam-Webster enlightens us with the definition: Strength or force gained by motion or by a series of events.

Strength and force gained by movement. Once you begin moving, then moving becomes easier. Remember Isaac Newton. An object in motion stays in motion unless something else stops it or gets in its path. Something like that. I wasn't paying that much attention in Physics. Think about that one thing on your "someday" to do list that makes you cringe…and then do it. Face it, dead on. Trust me, by the time you conquer that task, you're going to feel like a superhero.

Priorities. Some of us have them, some of us don't. And some of us have them, but they are way off the mark. You can tell by looking at our daily lives. People without priorities or who don't have very good ones find themselves in a situation like Caroline every single day. While these little daily choices may seem harmless in the short-term, you'll realize that cumulatively, they're quite harmful in the long-term, when you look up months, even years down the line and see that you haven't progressed in your life.

Considering your big goals, and your small chores, make a to-do list of everything you need to accomplish this week, and then number everything with ten being of the most importance and zero being of no importance. Then, start each day with a ten. Once you accomplish everything that is a ten, move on to nine, and so on. The zeros, you can probably just scratch off your list…

# CHAPTER 3:

## THE DIRTY "S" WORD

Self-discipline ain't easy, yet it is absolutely necessary for success. Think of a child. They have little self-control, so without an adult to walk them through things, they often will not have enough self-discipline to accomplish tasks that they don't want to complete. Unfortunately, some people never grow out of this. They might not consider going to bed early enough to get enough sleep, despite having an important appointment the next day. Or, they might procrastinate and not prepare that big presentation until the night before.

As adults, we have to be responsible for our own self-discipline, whether it is in how we manage our time, our projects, or our finances. We've already seen that Caroline has a hard time managing her time, but Matt has a hard time using self-discipline with his finances. Let's go back to our pal, Matt.

Matt not only has a mortgage on a house much larger than his tiny family needs that's located in a fancy neighborhood, but he also insists on having the latest expensive luxury cars. That's right *cars*. With an "S." A Range Rover for him, a Mercedes for his wife, and a BMW for his kid…who's eight. We all know the BMW is also for Matt. While he would like to leave his job and get away from his stressful boss and coworkers, Matt just can't afford to give his dream career a chance. He knows that being an entrepreneur can be highly profitable, but he also knows it takes time, time that he can't afford with his current high-end lifestyle. So what's a guy like Matt to do?

**Conquering Yourself**

It is important to remember that we always have choices. I know that life can sometimes put us in situations that make us feel like we are up against the wall with no way out. I don't know about you, but I don't want to let these circumstances get in the way of my dreams. I don't want them to get the better of me.

What you do with the hand that you are dealt with will inevitably correspond with the outcome of your life and the impact that you have on the lives of those around you. The people who get dealt a bad hand over and over, yet keep playing, refusing to give into failure, are the people who succeed and bring color to the world.

Stop telling yourself that you can't accomplish your goals. Getting your shit together…it's a slow process, man. So don't be afraid to start slow. Take that first step even if you are afraid of stumbling or have stumbled before. Every single person messes up and falls down. Not a single person you have met in your life is perfect, not even the people who look perfect are perfect. In fact, they can be the most messed up ones. But, it doesn't matter if you fall down as long as you get right back up and start swinging again.

Start small by doing what you know is easily possible for you—when it comes to your goals. If you have a goal of making a million dollars in revenue with your new business you started or want to start, start off with making your first dollar, then your first $100, then your first $1000, your first $10,000, and just gradually go up from there. The further you go, the easier it will be to see the top and the easier it will be to believe that you can get there. Don't worry if you can't see the top of the mountain from where you are, just get moving. You're not even supposed to see the top from where you are. If you can, you're dreaming too small anyway.

The people who reach their full potential are the ones who didn't stop when things got hard. They didn't let fear hold them hostage, pain hold them down, or laziness hold them back. Feed the fire inside of you and don't let it die. Don't be afraid to take risks or put yourself out there and go after what you want. This may mean you have to sacrifice time or money from other aspects of your life, but if it gets you to your goal, isn't it worth it? The difference between the people who make it and the people that don't are the people who fight for it and the people who won't.

## A Word To The Wise—Take The Words From The Wise

Are you sick of the nagging? From your mom or dad? Maybe that annoying aunt won't stop putting her two cents in when you didn't ask for it. Well, sorry to say this, but it's time to start asking. Or at least listening. The idea that being wise comes with age or experience is real. People older than you have had several more years to eff up their lives worse than you have until they stumbled around in the dark long enough to find the light switch. They nag because they care and they nag because they know.

While family can definitely have the wrong idea at times, no harm is done by listening and considering that what they're telling you is coming from a good and genuine place. You might not need to take the advice of your uncle who still lives in your grandparents' basement, showers bimonthly, and twitches at the sound of a bag of potato chips being opened, but I would listen to the advice of your older sister who's married to the love of her life and travels the world while running her lucrative online business. And advice doesn't have to come from relatives. It can come from friends, from famous entrepreneurs and other successful people, or from me. Wink ,wink. But, you can't just listen. Also act, dammit.

I like to play a little game called *not making things harder than they have to be*. In this very fun game, I take whatever situation I happen to be in and find the easiest way to handle it. What easier way to success is there than taking information from someone who has already been through the same thing or something similar? From someone who knows what they are talking about and has succeeded? From someone who has already successfully done what you want to do?

We learn from our mistakes, it's true. But, what if I told you that you don't always have to do things the hard way. Instead of learning from your own mistakes, you can save some pain and suffering and begin to learn from the mistakes of those around you. Take the shortcut. Let go of the idea that there's more glory in fumbling around, struggling, and figuring things out on your own. Take the easy way out, and learn from those that were before you.

## Create Your Habits Because Your Habits Are Creating You

I used to have a terrible habit. Any time something big and stressful was headed my way, I would head straight into a panicked *"what if"* and worst case scenario mode.

The thing is, I didn't used to know that about myself. It actually took me many years to realize what I was doing. Everywhere I turned, without fail, I was self-sabotaging myself. If it was a job change, needing to move locations, trying to do something I had never done before, or just trying to accomplish something under a time constraint, my brain would go off with whistles and alarms screaming *"This is bad. Shit. This is going to be so, so bad."* Yet, by the time I'd gotten to the end of whatever it was, not a single one of the things I had feared turned out as badly as I had made myself believe. Not a single one of them had even happened.

You'd think I'd eventually learn my lesson. But nope, seeing things actually turn out alright despite my convictions to the contrary, never prevented me from freaking out again. Freak out mode just wouldn't stay away. It wasn't until not just one person, but over time, several people asked me, *"Why do you do that? Why do you make everything so much worse in your head when you don't even know how things are going to turn out? Why are you freaking out when what you're freaking out about is probably never going to happen?"*

Good freaking question. Why did I do that?

Habit. We all have habits, both good and bad. Illogical freak out mode was one of the mental habits that I didn't even realize I had, yet, it was extremely powerful. This habit controlled how I approached new things, or *if* I approached new things. I was always terrified that something bad was going to happen to me. It's definitely not the type of habit that does anyone any favors.

One day, I decided that not only do I not want to live my life in pessimistic anticipation, but I also don't want to stress out and make myself miserable over unavoidable changes in a world where everything changes all the time. It was damn well time to make a change. How do you break an awful habit that is so ingrained in you that you didn't even realize that it was a habit?

You consciously change your thinking. Emphasis on the *consciously*. Our minds are endlessly having unconscious thoughts. Things are just constantly popping into our heads without us even realizing or trying. Whenever you have a negative *the sky is falling* thought pop into your head, stop yourself dead in your tracks, and tell yourself the opposite. Eventually, your brain will stop going immediately to the negative, and it will begin to develop a habit of optimism.

## The Devil On Your Shoulder

You know what you are supposed to be doing right now. You told yourself that you were going to go to the gym. But that ice cream in the freezer was unfortunately yelling your name louder than the gym was, so here you are, in the middle of your workout session, stuffing your face with Moose Tracks, catching up with your fave—*Grey's Anatomy*. During commercial breaks, you get on Facebook and see a meme that says "Didn't go to the gym today, but the cashier's name at McDonald's was Jim. So, you know, it's the same thing." You think it's funny. It's not.

When are you going to stop acting on impulse and start being deliberate with your actions? You can say that you have a goal to go to the gym and get in shape and actually do it or you can whine about how you need to get back in shape and then not do anything about it. You can't, however, do both.

Curb your unproductive impulses with understanding and acknowledging them. But, where do these impulses come from?

Sigmund Freud's theory of personality shows us a three-part system in which our instincts, reality, and morality combine to create a complex personality. Understanding this theory may help us understand our impulses and how to control them. According to Freud, some of these aspects are more primal, pressuring us to follow our base urges as mammals. Then, there are other portions of our personalities that develop over time, the purpose of which is to balance out our base urges.

- **The Id: (Instincts) The Devil On Your Shoulder.**

This is the only portion of our personality that, according to Freud, is present from our birth. The Id includes our base desires and instincts and is completely unconscious. This is because it is driven by the pleasure principle, therefore, it wants us to immediately satisfy our wants, needs, and desires. We are born with this portion of our personalities because it helps infants survive. Because of the Id, babies will cry and alert us when they are hungry, scared, or uncomfortable in any way. Because babies are ruled by the Id, we are unable to reason with them without meeting their needs.

- **The Ego: Reality.**

According to Freud's theory, the ego develops from the Id in order to help us express our impulses and needs in a socially acceptable manner. Since, ya know, going into a crying fit because you're hungry at age 30 just doesn't have the same effect on people as it does when you're a newborn. The ego functions not just in our unconscious mind, but also in our preconscious and conscious, as well.

Using the reality principle, the ego attempts to satisfy our needs and desires in appropriate ways by weighing out the costs and benefits of our actions before we decide what to do, rather than relying on pure impulses. In many cases, the ego can help us put off our needs until an appropriate time and place by being satisfied with delayed gratification.

- **The Superego: (Morality) The Angel On Your Other Shoulder.**

As we age, we develop the superego from influences such as our parents or guardians and society. The superego contains all of our learned moral standards of right and wrong, which we then use to help us make decisions. According to Freud, this portion of our personality begins to show at age five, but continues to develop into adulthood.

Freud concluded that there are two separate portions of the superego: the ideal and the conscience. The ideal portion of the superego contains the rules and standards we know for behaving well. Obeying these rules makes us feel good. We feel pride and a sense of accomplishment.

On the other hand, the conscience portion contains information that we have learned is wrong or have seen in a bad light. If we do one of these actions anyway, despite feeling and knowing that it's wrong, we will later feel a sense of guilt and remorse. The purpose of the superego is to perfect our actions, to suppress anything that the Id may want us to do that is unacceptable, and to influence the go-to act in accordance to idealistic standards. The superego is also present in our unconscious, preconscious, and conscious mind.

It is important, Freud stresses, to remember that while separate, the Id, Ego, and Superego are still interconnected. They are constantly interacting in a dynamic manner, in order to influence our behavior and personality. Yet, with these three different competing elements, we can sometimes struggle to know how to act. But, if we have a strong ego, we will more easily be able to function and decide which actions to take.

So to recap, the Id is the part of the psyche that is responsible for our basic animalistic instincts, and is where our impulses stem from. Our Ego is how we perceive the world around us and it helps us satisfy the needs of the Id in a healthy manner. The Superego helps not only control the impulses from our Id, but helps our ego choose the morally correct choice rather than a choice that is simply realistic.

Why is it important to understand these three conceptual parts of the personality? The Id may be responsible for the birth of our impulses, so yes, it can feel like we have no control over our impulses. But, our Ego is formed by how we decide to see the world around us. Our Superego is based off of our Ego and is the part of our personality that helps steer us toward making the correct choices and acting the right way. We control how we see the world around us, and with our superego, we are ultimately in control of our impulses.

How do we manage those pesky impulses that we have been unable to control in the past?

Let's take a look at some of the factors that weaken our ability to control our impulses so that maybe you can identify what your particular struggle is and be able to overcome it. This goes back to what we were discussing in an earlier section—the idea of willpower being a limited resource.

Shahram Heshmat, who works at the University of Illinois as an Associate Professor of Public Health & Economics, explains that when our willpower becomes tired, just like a muscle, we become more likely to act on our impulses from our Id. While we may regret it later, we become more likely to give in to desires and cravings. For instance, if you're on a diet and have had a really stressful day, constantly having to exert self-control, then you are more likely to give in to your cravings and show that half gallon of Cookies and Cream who's boss as soon as you get home.

Dr. Heshmat concludes that five key factors can lead to impulsive reactions due to weakened willpower.

- **Ego Depletion:** Making a series of decisions that involve conflict, trying to impress others or responding kindly to rude behavior can lead to ego depletion. Ego depletion is what leads to a loss of motivation.

- **Busyness:** The busier people are, the more likely they will behave impulsively. Also, when we are stressed, we can often forget little things we should know like the names of people, even if we know them well. When our mind is busy with stress, the short-term portion of our brain guides our choices.

- **Stress:** Coping with stress involves using willpower to control behavior. Regular daily stress will reduce the functioning of the prefrontal cortex, which is the portion of the brain that controls executive function, concentration, decision making, and judgment. As a result, our ability to use prudence and reflect on the impact of our decisions is reduced. We begin to function on default, rather than carefully considering our options.

- **Alcohol:** Because, obviously, alcohol impedes brain function.

- **Blood Sugar:** Glucose is a vital part of willpower. Evidence shows that exerting willpower can even lower our blood sugar levels, which reduces our capacity for self-control. Your brain uses about 20 percent of the energy your body consumes. Let's say you're on a diet. The caloric restriction common to most diets produces low levels of glucose, which will then undermine the willpower needed to resist excess food intake. Kind of ironic, isn't it?

You may not want homework, but I am going to give you some anyway. If you are reading this book, then you are determined to improve your life and reach your goals, and this homework will help you get there.

Take a good hard look at yourself and your patterns. Analyze which impulses you need to control. What factors could be weakening your ability to control them? Could it be that you haven't flexed your impulse control muscles in a while so they are weak, or that you are constantly running twenty-four/seven with no chance for rest?

Understanding what is weakening our ability to control ourselves and curb our impulses will help you with your plan of attack to keep yourself out of the vicious cycle that landed you here reading this book in the first place. At the end of the day, it is important to remember that even if it seems like we can't always necessarily control the impulses we have, like willpower, impulse control is a learned behavior that strengthens over time as we use it.

## Who Has It, Who Doesn't, And Why It Doesn't Matter

There is a popular misconception that you need to eliminate from your brain. It's the idea that it takes extreme beauty, brains, or talent to really be someone or do something with your life.

Beautiful people every day get into drugs, drop out of school, and ruin their lives attaching themselves to the wrong people. Incredibly intelligent people do dumb things like drink and drive, and get arrested. Extraordinarily talented people settle for minimum wage jobs with long hours and no future, and you'd never know they have it in them to be the next Picasso, or Beyonce, or Obama. So looks, smarts, and skills mean nothing and get you nowhere if you don't truly believe you're capable of achieving more. This is very good news for you if you're ugly, dumb, and inept.

What can really make the difference is pure determination. Someone can be born with beauty. Others can be born with amazing intelligence. And, someone can be born with talent. But, not a single one of these people are born with determination.

Determination stems from one thing and one thing only, and that is your will to never give in and never give up. Your will to carry on despite the setbacks, the excuses, and the failures which you have experienced. It's your will to keep going when every single other person in your position would quit. You need to read these words very carefully. They came from one of our most beloved horror writers of all time, Stephen King:

*"You can, you should. And if you are brave enough to start, then you will."*

In Stephen King's book, *The Craft*, he explains what happened when he received a rejection letter when he was only a kid. He placed a nail in the wall, and he stuck the rejection letter on it. By the time he had reached age fourteen, the nail had so many rejection letters on it that it would no longer support their weight, so he replaced it with a new nail. Still, he continued to write and submit his work. While this must have been discouraging, by the time he reached sixteen, the rejection letters began to be more encouraging, as they contained small little notes from the agents who wrote them.

He submitted one of his first novels, *Carrie*, to a publisher and they told him they were not interested in it, that they didn't believe it would sell. You know what then happened? No, it wasn't picked up by the next publisher. Or even the publisher after that. Or the one after that. In fact, it was turned down by thirty publishers before anyone was willing to give it a chance. But once Stephen finally got that chance, as we all know, the rest is history, as he is now widely regarded as one of the biggest literary legends of our time. He's published more than fifty novels. All best sellers, all across the globe. I bet those publishers that sent him all those rejection letters are feeling pretty stupid right about now.

Now, I can't think of a single thing in my life that I kept up after being told no, not once, or twice, or three times, but thirty freaking times. I probably shouldn't be telling you that since as the writer of this book, I'm supposed to be pumping you up. But that is the kind of pure determination that you need to succeed.

No one said it would be easy, did they? But, things that are worth it seldom come easy. There will be days that you stare at the ceiling, feeling like all you ever do is take one step forward and five steps back. You may have a lot of these days before you actually start to see progress. Yet, I can promise you one thing. It is there. Your opportunity is right on the other side if you just don't give up on yourself and don't allow yourself to think that you're not going to be successful because you weren't born hot enough, smart enough, or gifted enough. Let determination by your gift. It looks good on you, too.

Bragging on the internet can sometimes be a good thing.

This is one of those times.

Leave a review, bragging about how awesome you are for reading this book.

★★★★★

# CHAPTER 4:

## PROCRASTINATION NATION

You see procrastination everywhere. You know it's a universal issue by the countless jokes and memes about it all over the internet and social media. Yet, it is an actual serious problem. While you can make procrastination into a joke and laugh about it, if you truly want to succeed, you need to overcome your procrastination tendencies.

**It's Not Just You**

Raise your hand if you have ever procrastinated. You don't have to be shy, go ahead and raise it. You aren't the only one who procrastinates, you can trust me on that. I promise you that we are all guilty here. Whether it's pushing off studying for an exam, or pushing off taking care of that oil change, I think we can all confirm that we are oh too familiar with the realm of procrastination. Sometimes, we even procrastinate with things we *want* to do, such as eating or getting up to get the remote to change the channel, because more than we want to do those things, we *don't* want to get off the couch.

Here is what we know about procrastination, if you put off studying for that test you have coming up, you are increasing your chances to fail it. If you put off changing the oil in your car for too long, it will damage your engine. We know that the negative repercussions of procrastination tend to outweigh the pleasure of whatever activity is currently bringing us instant gratification. Yet, we still do it. Why?

Doctors Joseph R. Ferraria and Dianne M. Tice have conducted studies on procrastination. In two of these studies, the doctors studied a combined 147 people. The participants were asked to rate their levels of regular procrastination. They were then told, in a lab setting, that their performance would be tracked during a math test. They were also allowed to either practice the test or engage in fun activities, such as video games, if they wished, for fifteen minutes.

In the first of the two studies, the participants spent an average of 60% of their time procrastinating rather than working on math—well, I mean, who can blame them. In the second study, the exact same math test was presented as a fun game. The results showed that the people who initially rated themselves high on the procrastination scale did not procrastinate any more than the non-procrastinators. The results of both studies concluded that when a task is described as difficult and important, people are more likely to procrastinate, rather than if it is described as a fun task. This also led the researchers to conclude that procrastination is an unintentional self-imposed handicap, that many people may not even be aware that they have. So, the secret to ending procrastination? Brainwash yourself to believe that the things you need to get done are fun.

Procrastination is a self-defeating behavior. Yet, like other behaviors, they can be relearned if you are willing to examine yourself and discover how to replace that behavior with something better. Replace it with a habit that allows you to be productive rather than constantly setting yourself up to fail. All procrastination does is make you feel shitty about yourself and keep you from your goals in the long-run.

Although some people may know this, it can be hard for them to stop this self-destructive behavior, even if they know they need to. This is most likely because while most people will reassess their approach if their current method fails, people who have a chronic case of procrastination seem to develop a faulty feedback loop. They know that procrastination sucks, but because it offers short-term relief from stress, the brain begins to procrastinate frequently. While the person may know it is not the best choice, they reason it out because it always offers a short-term resolution to their negative emotions. Just as a night of drunken partying might distract you from a breakup, but only provide a hangover and regret, procrastination works in the same way.

Now that we have some insight as to why we keep getting stuck in that icky rut, we can look for the silver lining. We now understand that procrastination is enabled by our inability to deal with long-term versus short-term situations. The next step is to figure out how to defeat that line of thinking.

A study led by Dr. Fuschia Sirois of Bishop's University explored the factors that go into a person's likelihood of procrastination. Dr. Sirois believed that the cause of procrastination is due to the procrastinator's focus on regulating their emotions in the short-term, by doing tasks that make them feel better. Therefore, she believes that if a person is more empathetic with their future self, they will feel psychologically closer to that future self, helping them to make a better decision, and avoid procrastination. It sounds a little weird, but stay with me. Here's an example of putting this idea into action. Let's say someone is being extra levels of douchebag and says something unforgivable and greatly offensive to you. Sure you want to punch them in the face and peel off their eyebrows, but you resist because you empathize with the consequences for your future self. Yet, if you hear someone say an equally hurtful thing to a loved one, you are less likely to think about the long-term consequences of resorting to violence for that future self, and are more likely to punch the person in order to defend your loved one.

In another finding of this study, Dr. Sirois concluded that people who first visualize their future selves in a positive mindset completing their task are more likely to feel motivated to attain that satisfaction. If people visualize not completing the task and feeling bad about not succeeding, they may complete the task, but they experience more negative emotions related to it. Imagining succeeding rather than losing increases positive feelings, reduces stress, and results in a larger degree of motivation. More motivation = less procrastination.

Get in front of your thoughts and then change your mindset. What is it that you are telling yourself while on the brink of putting all of that crap you need to be doing on the back burner? Rather than thinking that you might fail, or worse ignoring your problems and to do's, take a minute and imagine yourself in the future. Imagine yourself succeeding and how good that will feel. Trust in yourself that you can make it happen, and then do it.

## Don't Live With It, Deal With It

I have to tell it to you straight. Because we're friends. And I'm honest with my friends. Most of the time. So here goes. Developing your self-discipline habit is doable, but it ain't easy. Just like any time you are learning any new skill, or breaking an addiction, it will be hard at first. Then, it's also hard the second time around, and the third time, and possibly a few dozen times after that. The good news, however, is that the more you get your body and your mind adjusted to an alternative way of doing something, it *does* get easier.

Drs. Wendy Wood, David Neal, and Jeffrey Quin, very important scientists at Duke University, conducted a study on habits—those behaviors and dispositions we go to automatically due to behaving in the same manner in the past. Habits will often keep people doing the exact same thing they have always done, even if they are trying to change. In fact, these researchers found that our habits account for an average of forty percent of our actions and behavior.

While this may make changing habits seem difficult, it is entirely possible. Remember, addictions are not just habits, but there are chemical compounds involved that compel people to continue the given addiction, whether it is alcohol, drugs, or anything else. Yet, every day, there are people who are living sober lives despite their addiction. They have been able to resist addiction, overcome it, and create new habits. If people can overcome addiction, then you, too, can build new habits for a better future and a better self.

Here's a few tips that will help you not only break your old habits, but build new ones. You can teach an old dog new tricks.

- **Substitute Habits**

    While bad habits, such as smoking or procrastination, have bad consequences, they also provide a sense of stress relief. In order to fully break a bad habit, it is then best to replace it with a good one. For instance, if you find yourself constantly running to the fridge to nibble on brownies when you should be working…well, first of all, stop.

    And second of all, do something else instead every time you get that urge, like 10 pushups or whatever positive replacement your pretty little head can come up with. If you are just trying to remove a bad habit, you will begin to obsess over it, making it more difficult to use willpower to fight off the urge. But, if you replace it with a new action, not only will it distract you from your old tendencies, but soon enough, you will have a healthy and productive habit that is just as powerful and impactful as your previous bad habit was.

- **Remove Triggers**

Just like an alcoholic shouldn't go to a bar, if you are trying to break a bad habit, you should avoid putting yourself in situations that make it easy for you to give in. If you are constantly looking at social media at times when you're supposed to be being productive, don't keep 12 tabs open in your browser with each of your social media accounts there waiting for you. Or better yet, download a social media blocking plug-in that will block all social media during your work hours. If television is your personal form of crack, then when it comes time to get work done, do your work in a room that doesn't have a TV. If you make it more difficult to follow through with a bad habit, you are less likely to go out of your way to give in to the urge. After all, we are naturally lazy. Learn to use it to your advantage.

- **Start Small**

If willpower is like a muscle, it can be stated that many people struggle when they try to lift too much—or in this case, change too big of a habit. These people simply don't have a strong enough willpower "muscle." They use it all up, and then when they are weakened, they give in. Therefore, it is best to start with small habits.

If you are a writer, rather than telling yourself to write five-thousand words a day, maybe start with one-thousand. Just pick a number that you find attainable. Smaller goals take less motivation, so you are more likely to succeed. As another example, it's much easier to eat one less scoop of ice cream than to completely cut it out of your diet. These small steps will also strengthen your willpower "muscle," making more difficult changes in the future easier to accomplish.

- **Slowly Increase**

Gradually increase your short-term goals to help you get closer to your long-term goals. Sounds easy enough, right? Taking the example from earlier, if you have a long-term goal of writing five-thousand words a day, but you currently have the attention span of a toddler in a Toys R Us, start with a smaller short-term goal of writing one-thousand words a day, and when you find success with that, then try increasing it gradually by two-hundred or five-hundred words until you get to your goal of being a regular Shakespeare…on steroids.

- **Visualize Success**

Remember Jim Carrey? Remember the Duke University study we just talked about that proves the efficacy of visualization tied to willpower? So, visualize yourself crushing it! You'll make it a heck of a lot easier on yourself when trying to break bad habits. Make a vision board. Or, if you're afraid of getting made fun of by your friends (or yourself), just close your eyes and see it in your mind. Professional athletes are known to do this to improve their performance during both practice and game time. Golf players visualize themselves making the perfect swing. Basketball players see themselves sinking baskets. If it works for top athletes, surely, it will work for you.

- **Get Back Up**

Nobody is perfect, and therefore, everyone fails at times. While you might be able to break an old habit and create a new one without failing from time to time, I hate to burst your bubble, but lightning won't strike every time—you will fail. How's that for a motivational book? Well consider this. While you don't want to exactly plan for failure (remember to visualize success), you do want to consider what might get in your way, and what you will do in case something does get in your way or you fall off the wagon.

For instance, if you are trying to give up sweets, then plan in advance what you will do in case someone offers you some cake, or a box of your favorite donuts pops up in the breakroom. While it is possible to fall off the wagon, remember, you've got this. You can always get back on. Even if you do happen to mess up once or twice, you shouldn't get down on yourself. Studies have shown that falling short of your goal occasionally when trying to create a new habit has little to no effect on the final outcome. Whose studies, you ask? Mine.

- **Be Patient**

You can't make progress if you are constantly berating yourself for not making progress fast enough. You're setting yourself up for a hard time if you expect instant results. This will simply cause you to stress and lose motivation. Remember, progress takes work, time, and patience. If you feel like it is taking too long to reach your goal, try to create more short-term goals to slowly help you work towards your long-term goal. Meeting the short-term goals more frequently will help you see your progress and encourage you to keep up the positive habits that are accumulating towards your success.

For instance, if someone is trying to lose 100 pounds, it's probably not going to happen overnight. If you have short-term goals of losing five pounds at a time, then you can frequently see the actual progress you are making, which will mentally keep you going. But remember, losing 100 pounds, even if only five pounds at a time, will still not happen overnight. Patience, my friend, patience.

- **Surround Yourself With Like-Minded People**

If you are trying to reach a goal or start a new habit, try to connect with people who are on the same course as you. This means they are also trying to reach your same goal, or even better, they are on the path ahead and have already reached it. Not only can these people give you tips, but just seeing other people succeeding and being encouraging can motivate you to keep on pushing. In fact, if you can't find people to surround yourself with in real life, cyberspace can be a perfectly swell alternative. One study found that people in a Facebook diet group had a much higher chance of succeeding in staying on their diet than those who took the solo route.

- **Reward Yourself**

All work and no play makes Jack a dull boy, and the same could be said for trying to build or break habits. If this process is all work, you can become tired, defeated, and lose all the strength in your willpower "muscles." Try to reward yourself for reaching goals. If you're a writer and your goal is to write one thousand words a day, then whenever you reach your goal, reward yourself with something. It could be a glass of wine, your favorite chocolate, allowing yourself the time to sit down and watch a TV show, whatever.

Think of some rewards you can give yourself each time you succeed (so long as they are rewards that don't derail your goals or success). As we mentioned in an earlier part of this book, not only does this feel good, but the positive reward will help rewire your brain, telling it that your new habit feels good. This then ingrains it in your brain, making it more natural and effortless.

- **If All Else Fails: Fine Yourself**

If you find that no amount of positive reinforcement is helping, then it may be time to pull out the big guns—the big, mean, ruthless guns.

Maybe it's time for a little *not so positive* reinforcement. Also known as punishment. To make this most effective, it is helpful to have someone else holding you accountable. Tell them your plan and ask them to ask you about your progress. In this method, you set up an amount of money you fine yourself with each time you fail and succumb to your bad habit.

A lot like a swear jar, simply place a fixed amount of money in the jar each time you do what you said you wouldn't. So, if you are giving up swearing, and as soon as you get in your car, you explode into a litany of every four-letter word ever known to man at the first person who makes you miss the greenlight, you're going to have to put some money in the jar. Actually, you're going to have to put *a lot* of money in the jar. You might just need to go ahead and get a second jar.

And in order for this self-imposed punishment game to work, the cardinal rule is that you're not allowed to collect all the money and then deposit it back into your bank account. You can, however, give this money to charity and support people who are stable enough to not go around cussing people out…unlike some people I know…

## Bite-Sized, Not Pint-Sized: How To Chew What You Are Biting Off

Have you seen a four-year-old go into a complete fit at a toy store when they're told they can't have the *Barbie Fashionistas Ultimate Closet Set*? They kick their legs, flail their arms, jump out of the shopping cart, throw themselves on the ground, and let out sounds that would make you think their parents were peeling their skin off, all while invoking judge-y stares from fellow nearby shoppers.

A meltdown due to overwhelm can provide a similar experience. Meltdowns are tiresome, and if you bite off more than you can chew, you are moments away from your very own crying, snot-dripping, and anxiety-invoking meltdown. Trust me, I am well acquainted with biting off more than I can chew. And I'm embarrassed to say that I have experienced my fair share of four-year-old-in-a-toy-store level meltdowns.

Unfortunately, there is a learning curve for this one. On one hand, you want to push your boundaries so that you can learn and grow. Yet, on the other hand, if you find yourself sleep deprived, isolated from social outings, drowning on current projects, and stretched thin, everything starts to feel hopelessly out of control.

How do you find the balance between the two?

Take a moment to really asses what you have going on right now in all aspects of your life. Write it all down so that you can see it plain as day in front of you. Are you juggling working and night school? A needy relationship, hobbies, family, and pet commitments? If necessary for your own physical health and mental sanity, you can say no to extra work shifts that come up, and you can say no to social invitations. It is important to be able to say "*no*" or "*not now.*" If people truly care about you, and you explain why you don't have time for something, then they should respect that.

But what if you already bit off more than you can chew and you are stuck in a precarious situation? Take a deep breath and get ready for some mental gymnastics. This is where prioritizing becomes important. Remember, you can split things up into two categories:

One: Shit that needs to be done ASAP.

Two: Shit that needs to be done, but can wait.

And you could also probably even add a Three: Shit that doesn't need to be done or needed to be done three years ago and I didn't do anything about and now it's been so long that I no longer can and this isn't relevant to my life anymore.

After you have that all sorted out, don't get wrapped up in your feelings. When we find ourselves in the

*"Dammit, how am I gonna get all of this done, why me?"* mentality we end up roaming in the land of procrastination and swimming in the ocean of neglected important tasks. As an alternative to being an unfruitful human, visualize yourself succeeding, and then make a plan on how you can get there.

Sometimes, just setting a timer for a half hour and just starting to chip away at that important task can help you make a dent in your project so it doesn't seem as big. Sometimes, that half hour is even enough to get it done.

Checking off your to-do list as you complete tasks can also be incredibly gratifying as you see the list of items you need to accomplish shrinking.

Make an action plan to blow through these as quickly and efficiently as possible. Don't be afraid to tell people that you are extremely busy and unable to take anything extra on for the next few days. If you have bitten off more than you can chew, then you don't have the extra time or willpower to be able to take on even more than you already have on your plate. If your friends try to give you a hard time and come at you with a *"Oh, so you think your little trying-to-make-your-life-better stuff is more important than getting grinded on against your will at the club while you babysit us due to our inability to contain our alcohol?,"* you can respond with a "yes." And if your friends come at you with a *"What, you think you're too good to hang out with us anymore?,"* you can say "yes." And then maybe get new friends.

What is the takeaway here? Sometimes, it is simply inevitable that you'll have a multitude of crap cascading down on you that demands your effort, time, and attention, and you'll have to get things done, even when it feels like your life is falling apart. In these cases, the word "no" is your best friend. You don't want to trigger a burnout. Or worse, a four-year-old-in-a-toy-store level meltdown.

## You're Never Going To Get There

Do you have a case of the Mondays? I don't mean *"Damn it all, it's Monday and I don't want to go to work…Is it Friday, yet?"* Not those Mondays…although that sucks too.

But what I mean is that you keep waiting to start that important thing that you need to do until Monday because it's a perfect sounding time to start.

*It is the beginning of the week after all, so no need to start something in the middle of the week, I mean, why would you do that? That's like leaving the TV volume on an odd number. It's just weird and it doesn't feel right. Plus, that'll make it easier when I'm tracking my weekly progress. Waiting for Monday only makes sense.*

But then Tuesday comes around and oh shoot—you forgot to start on Monday. So now you *have* to wait until the next Monday rolls around. Guess your life will have to remain in shambles for another six days. Oh well. Yeah, I know. I have been guilty of this as well. The same can often be said of New Year's resolutions as well. Let's see what my doctor friend has to say about this. He's not my friend, but he is a doctor.

Dr. Robert Holden, who founded *The Happiness Project*, defines a little something called "destination addiction" as a preoccupation or obsession that your happiness is always in the next place, one step ahead. "If I only had a better job," "if I only had a romantic relationship," "if I only had a bigger house," all of these thoughts and others, may be tied to destination addiction.

But the big, sad, ironic secret is that if we are unable to learn to be happy where we are, then we won't be happy even once we reach the goal that we worked for so diligently.

Dr. Holden explains that the trick to avoiding destination addiction is to love ourselves enough to want to succeed and be our best selves, but without waiting to live life for that moment. Live every moment of your life in a meaningful way that you can be proud of, rather than waiting for that someday. There is beauty and joy to be found in every life, whether someone is a successful entrepreneur, a stay-at-home parent, or a struggling artist. While you need to have a goal and willpower to reach that goal, don't let that goal override what is special in your life at this very moment.

Listen to me, you *will* make it. You don't, however, have to beat yourself up every step of the way. Positive reinforcement is so much more effective than a negative voice inside of your head yelling at you that you aren't good enough, telling you that this small victory or that small victory doesn't matter because you haven't made it to your end goal yet.

Because eventually, *"you aren't good enough"* or *"you haven't earned your happiness yet,"* is exactly what you'll believe. That mentality will never get you to where you want to go.

Take a deep breath and start being proud of yourself for putting your big kid pants on, all by yourself. Even if it's only for the smallest of your goals, if you accomplish something, then be proud of it. Be proud and own it. The minute you allow yourself to start enjoying the *now*, you'll realize that what you are working towards isn't so overwhelming or impossible to get to.

Do you want to look back on this next year and remember it as a dark time that you spent struggling to make something of yourself? Or, would you rather look back over the next year and be proud that yeah, you busted your ass to make something of yourself, and you accomplished something *and* enjoyed yourself while doing so? My vote is for the latter.

## You Are Amazing, Dammit

If you truly want something, darling, so badly that you can taste it, then there will be nothing and no one that can stand in your way except for you. There is no excuse you are unable to overcome. There is no reason that you can't work it out and make it happen. There is no person out there that you will believe when they tell you that you can't do it because you know you can. There will be absolutely nothing that can stop you, but you. Sure, circumstances might happen to try to get in your way, but as long as you never give up, then it is possible.

Past failures and mistakes only define you if you let them. The way I see it, you can tell yourself all the reasons that you can't. You can even justify those reasons by pointing out all the times that you failed before, but then you are ultimately just wasting your potential.

The person who you were yesterday, last year, or five years ago is only a stepping stone for who you are becoming and who you are going to be. All the challenges you have faced and all of the obstacles you have found yourself tripping over are only tools used to help make you stronger. You are the one who decides to choose to grow from your adversity or to let it defeat you.

You are capable of just as much as every person who has gone from dreaming to achieving. Every person's path is different. For some, that path is much more difficult, but decide right now that whatever comes your way, whatever happens, you can handle it. Decide that you won't let procrastination get the best of you and stop you from becoming your best self. Decide that you won't let your desire for comfort get in the way of your desire for success. Decide that you will turn your weaknesses into strength, your pain into growth, and your discomfort into the drive needed to push you further ahead towards your goals in life.

# CHAPTER 5:

## EFFECTIVE HUMAN BEHAVIOR

Whether you have always struggled with productivity, or if it is a new problem due to recent struggles that popped up in your life, this chapter will focus on several techniques you can introduce into your daily life that can help you learn to be more productive.

**Kiss Me, Fool**

A famous quote claims that *"simplicity is the ultimate sophistication."* While the identity of the original author of this quote is disputed, there is truth to it, nonetheless.

Entrepreneurs who specialize in productivity have regularly found that one of the most common mistakes that get in the way of being productive is something as simple as over-complication. One of the main keys to being productive and efficient is simplicity.

This has been well-known for a long time. In fact, the U.S Navy coined the term "*keep it simple, stupid*" in the 1970's, though it now has multiple variations, including "keep it sweet and simple." This sense of simplicity does not mean that whatever you are doing is simplistic, quick, or easy. Rather, it means using the most logical, clear, accessible, and…well, simple method to tackle a problem.

Think about this. In software, the best programming is coded in as simple of a manner as possible. This makes it easy to edit, it contains fewer errors, and it becomes easier for other people on a software development team to understand when needed. Not only that, but if it is a type of software to be used long term, it will be easier to maintain if written in a simple format.

A lot of people think that aiming for simplicity automatically means that they'll end up with the same solutions to problems as everyone else, but this is not true. Firstly, you are a beautiful snowflake and there is nobody in the world like you. You're my special little star. You're unique, ok? Secondly, the simple path is often less traveled. This is because most people have a tendency to overcomplicate things, can't wrap their heads around the fact that everything doesn't have to be pull-your-hair-out-in-clumps stressful and complicated, want the pride of feeling like they overcame something extremely difficult rather than easy, and they often associate simple concepts and solutions with being just plain boring.

I mean, do you *need* to spend 14 hours on that four-slide powerpoint presentation? Do you *have* to spend that extra time perfecting the vertical and horizontal alignment of every single line of text? Do you have to change that one line of 10.5 font to 10 font? Is it worth it? Is the outcome of all that extra work in proportion to the work put in? These are all rhetorical questions, by the way. But if these questions had answers, those answers would be no. Anyway, remember that few things are permanent or life-threatening, and most things are fixable. If you finish up that powerpoint and you feel it isn't snazzy enough for your ridiculous tastes, you can always spice it up later. But first, just get the dang thing done for crying out loud.

Here's another thought. In sports, the key to playing well is to hone the basics. A coach can train his team to learn a wide variety of plays and signals, but if they are unable to do the basics, then they will be unable to win. If you can't hit the ball in the right direction, if you can't run, if you can't catch, then you can have the most amazing one-handed, arm behind the back, under the leg, upside down trick move that you want and still fail.

The same is true for business, school, and any other areas of life.

Make a list of the fundamentals in your chosen profession, degree, or whatever other areas of life you are hoping to excel in. These fundamentals are the skills that you will need to use practically every hour and every moment that you are practicing your chosen field. If you are an artist, this could mean practicing your sense of depth perception, shading, and smooth strokes. If you are a novel writer, this means learning to convey emotion, world-building, and plot structure. If you are a baseball player, this could mean learning to hit a variety of pitches, assess what your opposition will do next, throw the ball to a teammate, and knowing when to stop running…and when to start.

Every chosen field has different fundamentals, and practicing these fundamentals and learning to excel in them will help you much more than learning fancy tricks ever will. Fancy tricks make great party tricks. But they're of no use when it comes to getting things done.

## Who The Heck Is Ivy Lee?

Do you want a simple method to easily become more productive, that you know will work? Well, then, the Ivy Lee method is for you. This method has been shown time and time again to help people from small business owners to large corporations. This has held true of the Ivy Lee Method for over 100 years.

In the year 1918, this simple but effective method took roots when Charles M. Schwab, one of the richest men at the time, was looking to boost efficiency for his company, the Bethlehem Steel Corporation. At the time, his company was the second-largest producer of steel in the U.S. and the largest shipbuilder.

In order to increase efficiency, Charles Schwab arranged a meeting with a well-renowned productivity consultant and businessman, Ivy Lee. After speaking with each of the executives in the company for only fifteen minutes, Ivy Lee developed a plan. When asked how much the consultation would cost, Lee replied "nothing, unless it works," and simply stated that Schwab could pay him however much he saw fit after a three-month test period.

Well, by the end of the test period, Schwab ended up writing Lee a check for $25,000, which is equivalent to over $400,000 today. So, it's safe to say that Schwab was happy with Lee's results.

## The steps are simple:

- Before bed at night, write down no more than six of the most important items that you need to accomplish the following day.

- After those items are written out, rewrite them in order of most importance to least importance.
- At the beginning of your day, focus on getting the first of the tasks, the most important task, finished before you do any of the others. Only after *completing* the first task, move on to the second task, and continue to work your way down the list.
- If you have any unfinished items from the day, simply add it to the list of items for the next day (while still keeping your list capped at six total items max).
- You then repeat this process on a daily basis.

Sound simple? Good. It's supposed to be.

**Tomato Time**

I love games. In my pre-productivity days, at my worst, I used to literally play video games until the sun came up. Now, I can't afford to do that anymore, but I love it when I can incorporate some kind of game in my daily life. Enter, the Pomodoro Method. "Pomodoro" is Italian for tomato, and rumor has it, the method was created using a tomato-shaped kitchen timer. Using this method, you can make a sort of "race against the clock" game out of productivity, turning something frustrating into something fun. This could be especially helpful for people who live with ADD or ADHD, whether medically diagnosed or self-diagnosed. Hey, either way, I'm not judging.

It works like this: rather than trying to focus on your task at hand for long periods of time, with the Pomodoro technique, you only have to focus on a single task for twenty-five minutes, and then you get to reward yourself! Doesn't that sound so much better than sitting at a desk, banging your head into your computer screen for ten hour straight. So, how does this work, exactly? I'm about to tell you, duh.

- Set a timer for twenty-five minutes, and see just how much work you can possibly get done during this time. Really try to race the clock and make it into a challenging game for yourself.

- After the twenty-five minutes, record your progress, so that later, you can track and see how much you improve over time. If you're writing, take note of your word count in the allotted amount of time, etc.

- After you complete the twenty-five minutes, reward yourself with five minutes to do whatever you please. This could be enjoying a cup of coffee, texting friends, ordering that Asian Man Wall Decal on Amazon, whatever you want to do that you can get done in five minutes.

- After four periods of working, you've now earned a longer break of fifteen to twenty minutes.

The Pomodoro Method. Making productivity fun again. Shall we make red hats? No. No, we shouldn't.

## The Upside-Down

Don't fear. This method is much safer than traveling to the Upside-Down in Netflix's *Stranger Things*.

Imagine that you're a failure. Hopefully, that's a stretch for you at this point in the book. I know, I know, this may seem counter to the ideas we discussed earlier, and it may feel like your very foundation has been shaken and you don't know what to believe anymore or who to trust, but bear with me. While visualization techniques usually increase motivation when you imagine yourself succeeding, there is still something to be said for something called "The Inversion Technique."

This technique is thousands of years old and originates from the Stoic philosophers, who regularly used this practice. In this method, the philosophers specifically imagined themselves failing. And they had terrific results, the idea being that if you take the time to imagine what could go wrong, then it gives you the opportunity in advance to address any possible issues and hopefully avoid mistakes. The steps for this method are quick and easy:

- Imagine the most important project you are currently working on or goal you are trying to attain.

- Visualize yourself ahead of time, after the project is over. But, imagine that you failed.

- Then, simply walk yourself through all the mistakes you could have made to get to that point of failure.

- Now, develop a plan and write down a list of potential ways in which you can avoid these problems. This way, if something comes up, you are prepared.

While this method can be used as a great, helpful tool, please don't let it take your mind into a spiral of anxiety. If you are someone who has an anxiety disorder or acts like it, this method might stress you out too much. Remember, you want to use this as a tool to prevent mistakes, but still have a positive and strong-willed outlook.

## But What If I'm Not A Morning Person?

You commonly hear the phrase *"early to bed and early to rise,"* which is a shortened version of a quote from Benjamin Franklin. The remainder of the quote goes on to say *"makes a man healthy, wealthy, and wise."* Another common quip that people enjoy quoting is *"successful people get more done before breakfast than most people get done in a day."* While this might be true, in a sense, that does not mean that you need to be an early riser to be successful and achieve your dreams. The opposite could probably also be said—night owls are toiling away getting work done while those early risers sleep and count sheep.

While Tim Cook, the CEO of Apple, may get up at 3:45 am, and while Oprah may get up at 5:45 am, there are many successful entrepreneurs and multi-millionaires who are just as successful, despite waking up later.

In fact, the CEO of Buzzfeed, Jonah Peretti, sleeps in until 8:30 am. This may not be considered "sleeping in" to a large majority of people, yet in the world of business, this is quite late. After all, this is nearly five hours later than Tim Cook, who's almost done with his day before Jonah even eats his breakfast.

A writer for the New Yorker and a TED talk speaker, Kathryn Schulz, has found that she is most productive during the middle of the night. In fact, her brain does not fully wake up to get ready for writing until 10 pm.

The former Prime Minister of England, Winston Churchill, did not have the luxury of sleeping in. Yet, he would remain in bed until 11 am each day. Until then, he would eat breakfast and work in bed.

The co-founder of Reddit, Alexis Ohanian, usually sleeps in until at least 10 am, and instead of an alarm clock, he relies on his hungry cat to wake him up.

The co-founder of the website *Genius*, formerly known as *Rap Genius*, Tom Lehman, begins his day the same way as many of us. He doesn't go to sleep until around 3 am, therefore, he often sleeps in until 10:30. The first thing he does in the day? He checks social media, including Twitter. I'm not recommending that last part, by the way. Know your limits.

These are just a few prime examples—all of which probably make a lot more money than you. So not only are there real-life examples proving that it is possible to be successful while not being a morning person, but there is also science that backs this principle up. You are not doomed to failure if the idea of waking up at 6 am, 8 am, or even 10 am makes you anxious and makes you want to press the snooze button.

It is estimated that fifty percent of the population is neither a morning person nor a night person, but rather they are somewhere in between. In today's society, it may be more common to succeed under this normalized schedule or a morning-centered schedule, but these are not the only roads to success.

Morning larks tend to achieve more academically, largely due to academic classes taking place earlier in the day. However, night owls have been shown to regularly perform better on tests of processing speed, cognitive ability, and memory. While this is most powerful in the evenings, they still rank higher in the morning times than morning larks. Night owls have also been shown to be generally more open to new experiences, more creative, and equally as healthy and wealthy. Take that, Mom and countless professors!!

A biologist from Oxford University, Katharina Wulff, has studied sleep and chronotypes extensively, making her an expert on whether or not it is truly better to be an early riser.

All of you night owls can breathe a deep sigh of relief (I just let out a big sigh) because Dr. Wulff has found that people naturally feel much better when they are left to wake up at their preferred times. When left to wake up when they want, not only do they not wake up in a murderous rage, but they are more productive, and their mental capacity is much better. She states that pushing people too far out of their natural preference, such as trying to make a night owl into a morning lark, can actually prove to be harmful.

This is because when a night owl wakes up earlier than their body believes they should, they are still producing the sleep hormone melatonin. This disrupts the body's natural cycle and pushes it into being in an inefficient daytime mode. This can have many negative consequences on both the mind and body, including increasing insulin resistance and causing weight gain.

Researchers have also found that our internal clock, the circadian rhythm, is largely biological. The cells that contribute to this internal clock are even produced largely in vitro, meaning that they are formed before birth and up to 47% of these cells are inherited from our parents. This is largely why it is common for people in the same family to all have the same sleeping habits, though there is sometimes an odd duck in a family with a sleeping schedule different from the rest.

One of the factors that affect the internal clock and therefore your sleeping schedule is a genetic component that affects the length of your internal clock. While most humans have a 24.2-hour internal clock, night owls have been shown to have a longer clock. This means that over time, they can begin to fall asleep later and later, therefore sleeping even later, as well. This has no outward cause, just the body thinking the day should be longer than it actually is.

If you, like me, have been confused because you were once a morning person and are now a night owl, this is also explained by the wonders of science. Oh, so many wonders of science. Your natural sleep preferences can change as you age. Children will naturally lean towards a morning schedule, whereas people in their twenties tend to have a later schedule, and then once people hit their fifties, they tend to revert back towards a morning schedule.

Those in academia are often taught this phrase: "correlation does not equal causation." In this case, that means that just because many successful people are early risers, it does not mean that waking early is the cause of being successful or that you *have* to wake up early in order to be successful. Rather, the reason waking early and success are often correlated is most likely because societal conventions like "work" and "school" often start early in the morning, requiring people to wake early. People who are naturally early risers will benefit from this system, whereas night owls will suffer while feeling groggily fatigued at a level where it feels like not even an intravenous injection of espresso will help.

Researches have also found that because night owls are often forced to have schedules that they are unable to easily maintain, they can be susceptible to lower moods and less satisfaction in life.

If all of that isn't enough to convince you that it's okay to sleep in, if your schedule will allow it, then read this. It has been found that when creative night owls try to become morning people due to peer pressure, they become less likely to create. Due to exhaustion, they not only don't increase in productivity in the mornings, but their level of productivity and creativeness decreases at later times that would normally be optimal for them.

Remember, "consistent action leads to consistent reward," so it is better to set yourself a schedule in which you can continuously be productive rather than one that makes productivity more difficult. If you are unable to get up before 8 am, don't sweat it. You should do what feels best and most natural for your body. Do you, boo.

**Tips For Getting Shit Done**

Overall, getting shit done as a morning lark is relatively similar to getting shit done as a night owl. It's just that one happens in the morning and the other at night. No matter your chronotype, here are some tips that may help you more easily find your road to success.

## Track Yourself

Even if you know you already know that you're a night person or a morning person, it is important to know exactly which points of the day you have the most energy and the least energy. For instance, I know that while I may be able to work before 10 am, if I do so, then I will only get about half of the work done. At most. I spend most of that working time in a lethargic state, unable to focus. I also know that after 1 am, my productivity tends to decrease, even if I am able to stay awake until 5 am.

Being successful as a night owl is largely about trying to find which times your brain and body can best perform to fit your lifestyle. Try to track these energy lulls and spikes. Write them down in your phone or a small notebook for a week, and then look for consistencies. While doing this, it can also help to find other factors that may affect your work.

Do you find that you can work better if you exercise first? Do you need to eat a mid-afternoon snack in order to focus? Does music help or hinder you? While the focus is trying to find your best working hours, tracking your productivity tendencies in general can be very helpful to aid you in discovering other aspects that impact your work, thus leading you to your own ideal set of circumstances for maximum productivity.

While some of these aspects are easiest to adjust if you are self-employed (or unemployed), there may be aspects that you can control at work, as well. For instance, I know a cashier who always avoids morning shifts and specifically requests the closing shifts. There are also people who may need a mid-afternoon nap in order to focus. If you have an office, this is easiest, as you can usually close the door during your break and get 15 minutes of Z's in.

But, I also know people who work manual labor jobs inside of an open layout building. To get an afternoon nap, they simply lay out a blanket and wear earbuds with music while they nap. If you drive, you can even pop over to the parking garage and get in your car for a quick nap. It may be weird getting used to sleeping at work in the beginning, but you will most likely adjust and find that soon, you will appreciate those quick moments where you can sleep peacefully to recharge for the remainder of your day.

## Love Yourself

While morning people often exercise, meditate, write in a journal, and eat well, it is important that you don't forsake these important self-care tasks just because you are forsaking mornings. These habits that promote health in both mind and body can be done at any point of the day, not just in the morning. In fact, many night owls have insomnia and can't shut off their brains. If you are one of these people, then meditating before bed might help your brain calm down so that you can sleep. Find the schedule that works for you, even if that means you are exercising at 1 pm or taking a nap at 7 pm.

**Structure, Structure, Structure**

If you are like me, then you recoil at the word "structure." Oh, Gosh, I just did it, I just recoiled. Yet, it is important to have some amount of structure. Before you get on social media for the day, try to either go over the Ivy Lee Method list you made the previous night of what you need to accomplish that day or create one if you were procrastinating...I'm giving you the side eye.

While you don't have to put something in a time slot for every hour or minute, you do need to know what needs to be accomplished and the general time you plan on doing it. If you do this first thing in the morning, before you even look at your phone, then you will start out your day productively.

You will start out thinking about your needs rather than what all is going on in the world. This can also be a boost to keep on pushing yourself to be productive, instead of wishing you could lay in bed looking at Instagram longer.

## Plan Ahead To Get Ahead

There is a common saying, which is "those who fail to plan, plan to fail." While you may not be actively planning on failing, if you fail to plan, you are much more likely to fail in meeting your goals. Rarely do people haphazardly throw spaghetti at the wall and become billionaires. This whole planning thing is helpful and necessary in many aspects of life, but especially in business. It is also worth noting that there are different types of planning. Before we explore how to plan, we will explore what type of planning you may need.

## Operational Planning

This type of planning is a guideline of how you need to accomplish a goal. This is often a step-by-step and day-by-day type of planning. It is a game plan either for running a company, running a household, or running an event. Operational planning is arguably the most beginner-friendly approach, as you simply write out a list of what you need to do for a specific day.

## Tactical Planning

When you are planning at the tactical level, you are planning out many short-term goals that you need to accomplish, whether for the week or for the month. If you have long-term goals from strategic planning, then tactical planning will help you know how to reach those goals. For instance, if you are planning an event, you may need to go shopping for supplies. In this case, shopping at various stores could be a part of your tactical plan, whereas the specific items you need to buy at that store would be on your operational plan.

## Strategic Planning

If you have big picture long-term goals, these are your strategic plans. This is all about creating a vision, a mission, and a goal at the highest level. This will include an overview of your entire business or another goal at the highest level, and the strategic plan will dictate the tactical plan and the operational plan. In this plan, you can include anything from within the next three years to ten years. For instance, if you want to have a certain salary or own a successful business, these would go on your strategic plan.

## Contingency Planning

Unexpected things happen, and the best way to deal with them is if we have a plan. We might not know in detail what could go wrong, but if we consider some of the possibilities, we can create plans that will counteract them. This is especially critical when you are working on a deadline or an incredibly important project.

An unexpected event you could plan for could be what you will do if you lose power or WiFi, what to do if someone goes into the hospital, if your computer breaks, if the price on a needed item increases, etc. That way, if these obstacles come up, they don't become excuses for you to stop working. For instance, one of my contingency plans for if the power or WiFi goes out is to drive up the road to Starbucks where I can still get things done, plus with an added bonus of being in close proximity to caffeine, treats, and sometimes a little eye candy.

A savings account is another form of contingency planning. I like to keep money aside in a short term savings account so that if something breaks that I need for my business, like my computer, I can replace it without worrying about impacting my regular budget.

While nobody wants to encounter these less than ideal situations, they are all too common. If you have a plan to deal with it, you will find that it will greatly reduce your stress, eliminate your potential excuses, and increase your chance for success.

Now that we have explored the main types of planning, let's get into the types of planners you may choose to use for this. While everyone has a favorite type of planning or even a favorite planner brand, these are some of the most commonly preferred types. Yeah, that's right—we're going deep with this. It may seem insignificant, but knowing what works best for you can be the difference between you achieving your goals and you wandering in metaphorical circles around the same level of mediocrity you've been at since the Spice Girls made that movie that nobody saw but me.

**Traditional Planner**

You can seldom go wrong with a traditional planner. They usually have monthly and weekly overviews, as well as daily pages. This means that you can use it for strategic, tactical, and operational planning.

These types of planners are also easy to find, with many different features. But, like when looking for someone new to date, look around online, in craft stores, and office supply stores to find what will work best for you, rather than picking the first one you find.

**To-Do Planner**

If you are a person who finds you get the most done with a simple to-do list, these planners are for you. They often simply have weekly and daily pages, or monthly and daily. They also often have designated times on them, so that if you need to do a certain task at a specific time, it is already written out for you. These are best used for operational planning.

## Financial Planner

Keeping your finances in order is important for any adult, but especially for people who are attempting to live on a budget, save money, or begin their own company—which, honestly, if you're doing life right, you should fall into at least one of those categories. Financial planners typically will contain sections for monthly and weekly bills and budgets. Some of these planners may even include traditional weekly and daily pages with areas to log expenses, bills, and financial goals. Some people find that having things like this written down is preferable to having them than an app like Mint. Or, you may prefer the $21^{st}$ century route and go strictly for an app. Or, you could be a hybrid and use both. But, everyone should have a financial plan in addition to a plan for the other goals in their lives.

## Bullet Journal

Planning with a bullet journal, the notebooks with the dot grids in them, has become all the rage. Something about dots on paper has recently taken the world by storm. Bullet journals are very versatile for planning or journaling, because it's...blank pages, so you can completely make it your own to fit your needs. However, without headings and subheadings for the various sections, or pre-filled dates, this type of planning will take much more time and creativity, since bullet journals do not have anything in them. You have to create every single thing yourself. Therefore, bullet journaling is best for creative people who have a little extra time to devote to their planner—make that *a lot* of extra time to devote to their planner. Check out the "Plan with Me" Youtube videos, and you'll see what I mean. If what you see makes you roll your eyes, curl up your facial expression to match that really judgmental looking emoji, or makes you sick to your stomach, bullet journaling is probably not for you.

But at the same time, while some people may use extensive creative and ridiculously detailed designs, it is not necessary. You can go with a basic minimalist approach, which will take much less time.

## Planning Tips For Success: Three Things To Add To Your Planner

- Add fun. Whether you enjoy hanging out with friends or spending time on hobbies, work it into your planner. Not only will this give you something to look forward to and motivate you to work harder, but as we discussed, having breaks helps to prevent burnout. Knowing that you have set aside time to do something enjoyable will lessen your stress.

- Add what you've already planned, and completed. Many people write down what they need to do, but don't keep a list of what they have already accomplished. While it may seem pointless to write down your accomplishments, it is far from that. First, if you begin to get overwhelmed or begin to have negative thoughts, you can look at all you have done up to this point in time and get inspired and motivated to keep moving forward. Secondly, when it comes time to create something like a resume, or proposal, you will already have a tremendous head start.

- Add planner time. Whether you set up your following day's plan before bed at night or wait until morning to schedule your day, be sure to set aside time at some point *every* day to quickly go over your planner and add any important information.

## Don't Skip The Little Things, They'll Come Back To Bite You In The Ass

Many of the mistakes we make that reduce our productivity and increase procrastination are seemingly small, but they actually make a big impact. Just making a few changes could change your way of life and business, decreasing stress, and increasing success.

Here's a summary of many techniques we've discussed that you can implement to make positive changes and boost your productivity:

**Create order.** One of the most common problems is to have a long list of items that need to be done, but doing them in a random or haphazard order. When you have a to-do list, similar to the priority ranking system we discussed earlier, pick the top three to five items that are most important to complete, and complete them before anything else on the list. This way, you don't end up accidentally putting off something important or missing an important deadline. After you finish these items, you can then move on to the remainder of your list.

**Separate your daily list from your weekly list, or rather your operational list from your tactical list.** If you have everything you need to do within the next week or two on one long list, not only does it make it harder to do the most important things first, but it also becomes overwhelming. And overwhelmed is not what we're going for. It's not a good look.

**Create mini-lists.** If you are someone who struggles with anxiety and self-doubt, this might help you. Along with your daily operational list, create mini lists for the various tasks you have to complete. For instance, if you run a blog, you can have a mini list of everything you need to do in order to create a blog post: writing, finding and editing a photo, adding tags, sharing it on social media, etc. You don't even necessarily have to write this list beforehand. There are many people who get overwhelmed easily who will write these lists as they accomplish items. So, if you have just finished sharing a post on social media, you can then write it down and immediately check it off. Doesn't that feel good? For people who are perfectionists, berate the hell out of themselves, or get stressed easily, this method can be incredibly encouraging.

**Build pre-work habits.** This can be especially helpful if you are a freelancer or work from home. If you are someone who has difficulty actually getting to work, try building habits that you always do before you begin work, so that it's easier for you to transition into starting your work, and so that you're more likely to feel motivated to work after completing these habits. This can be as simple as a habit of grabbing a coffee, doing yoga, or organizing your planner for the day. The idea is to create some sort of association in your brain between a certain task and doing work.

**Choose your soundtrack...or lack thereof.** Something that helps me personally when I work is listening to music—90s music being my personal fave. It helps prevent me from getting distracted and helps my work flow more smoothly. However, if you can't listen to a song without involuntarily singing and dancing like you're the sixth member of N'SYNC, listening to music while you work may not be a good idea for you.

You may want to listen to calming nature sounds or white noise instead. There are white noise machines, apps, and websites. If you like hearing rain, rushing rivers, or birds singing to you like you're a Disney princess frolicking in the forest, there's an app for that. Or the ambient sounds of the office, coffee shop, or at home might be more your vibe. There's an app for that too. Or maybe you need complete silence to work. Whatever sound you need (or don't need), just know and implement what works for you. But one sound, you definitely do not need while you're working is your cell phone. Be sure to silence it and remove it from your sight, or just completely put it away in a bag or leave it in another room.

**Track your missteps**. In order to become more productive, you need to know where you waste time. Every time you find yourself doing something other than work when you're supposed to be working, write it down in a notebook. After a week or two of tracking this, you should have a decent sized list. Go over it and find your most common issues. Once you know what distracts you, then you can more easily defend against it.

**Stop working at times**. As we've learned, not working is not always counterproductive, but it is important to not overwork yourself if you want to avoid burnout and give yourself opportunities to recharge your batteries. Technology makes it all too easy to stay connected and work around the clock, but you need time off. Teach yourself that after you have completed your hours or tasks for the day that you are done. You can do this by developing habits that will get you out of work mode, just the way you can create habits that can get you into work mode. For instance, many people will refuse to check their work email address after they are off the clock. And doing something calming such as yoga or making a cup of tea might also help.

**Keep fuel within reach**. Rather than having to waste time to get up and find water or a snack whenever you need refreshment, keep these things around your office or desk. You can easily keep a reusable metal water bottle nearby. Snacks such as almonds easily fit in a drawer. And my personal favorite, chocolate covered almonds, could be an extra special treat for after accomplishing a task on your list. You can even keep a thermos of hot or chilled coffee or tea nearby as well.

**Take many notes**. When talking with clients, coworkers, your boss, or anyone else in your profession, always have a way of taking notes on hand. Your go-to method for this will probably be an app on your phone, given that it's the $21^{st}$ century, but if you're old-fashioned and like paper, pen, #2 pencil, ink and feather…knock yourself out. But, taking note of things will ensure that you don't forget anything important that was talked about. Not only will this help prevent forgetfulness and therefore mistakes, but it will also help reduce wasted back and forth time since you won't have to ask someone again about something that has already been discussed.

**Keep an organized workspace.** A cluttered workspace not only leads to a cluttered mind, but it takes up valuable time. While you are busy trying to find that pen, important document, or stapler, you could be working. While it may seem small, these distractions can accumulate and get you out of your working groove, which it will then take more time and mental energy to get back into.

**Make a deadline, even if it's not needed.** Even if your project does not need a deadline, if you give yourself one, then you are much more likely to get it done. Hell, sometimes, I give myself a tight deadline solely to push myself to improve my working speed. Parkinson's Law says that tasks expand or contract to fill whatever allotted time they are given. So, if you give yourself three weeks to write that five-page manuscript, it will take you three weeks. If you give yourself three days, guess what? You're going to get it done in three days.

**Do what you say you're going to do.** Tell yourself you will start something, and then do it. If you are someone who has a difficult time finding the initial motivation to get started, then try giving yourself an impending start time. You can tell yourself that you will get started in one minute. Or three seconds. You can then either count yourself down or watch the clock. The trick is to not let yourself back out of it.

Once you tell yourself you will start at that specific time, you do it. Otherwise…well, it's not going to work. Mel Robbins, entrepreneur and motivational speaker, will count down from five before beginning a task she doesn't want to complete. You can use this tool to help you overcome bad habits and empower you to have control over your actions. Not only that, but as you succeed, you will feel a sense of accomplishment and therefore, most likely increased inspiration, pushing you to do more.

**Forgive yourself.** Everyone is bound to make mistakes, but holding on to mistakes, coupled with insistent perfectionism, will paralyze you and make you unable to move forward. I was plagued by this growing up. I really let that perfectionism control me. Eventually, I had to learn that if I wanted to reach my goals, I had to let perfectionism go. After all, we learn from our mistakes. Try to learn to let that overwhelming need to be perfect go, accept that you make mistakes, forgive yourself, and then try to improve based on your newfound wisdom. Perfect is lame. And it also doesn't exist.

**Consider hiring help, especially if you are an entrepreneur or freelancer.** When I was a kid, imagining my adult life, I always fantasized about being the person who would say *"I'll have my assistant follow up with you."* That would mean that I'd really made it.

Nowadays, with a little thing called the internet, having an assistant is easier than ever. You can get a virtual assistant to handle some of your smaller tasks, like helping you with emails, paperwork, and phone calls, to free up your time so you can focus on bigger picture items. Even if you only hire a virtual assistant for one or two hours a week, that is a couple of hours you can spend focusing on something else. And you don't have to limit your VA use to only work-related tasks. You can have a VA shop for your anniversary gift, plan a date night, or help coordinate arrangements for a trip. Anything you would do on a computer or a phone (which is most things), you could have a VA help you with.

## Checking Back In On Our Old Friends…

Remember Matt and Caroline? They've been reading this book, and now they've started to implement some of the techniques mentioned. By this point, Matt and Caroline have learned a lot. It is all still new and they are working on adjusting, but they've made great progress.

Matt has decided to take down the pergola, sell the BMW, and adopt a more frugal lifestyle altogether. He's been keeping track of all of his bills, weekly spending, and savings in his financial planner. And instead of throwing away the weekly sales papers that come in the mail, he actually clips coupons now, and saves money every week on the ingredients for that quinoa avocado toast his wife likes so much. Now that he isn't spending as much money on cars and quinoa, he has been able to start putting money aside to prepare him for the future. And rather than spending his off-time mindlessly, he's ditched the *Real Housewives of Orange County*, and is instead building robots with his kid every night, and making breakfast in bed for his wife every morning.

Before bed, every night, Matt makes a list of important tasks he has to get done at work the following day, and he adds to that list one thing he can do to get himself out of his job and closer to his dreams. Once he is done planning for the night, he meditates for a few minutes to help quiet his brain, allowing him to sleep better, which gives him the energy to perform better at work, and better deal with his annoying boss.

Matt has started a new habit of waking up earlier, which makes him feel less stressed, and helps him better prepare his kid for school when it's his week. No more Twinkies for breakfast.

Caroline has learned that she is a night owl, which does make her days with early morning classes more difficult, but she has learned that if she takes a mid-day nap, she can more easily keep up with the remainder of her day. She has taken steps to better organize her life, including setting aside time to plan, clean, and exercise for a few minutes each day. She doesn't have much excess time while trying to keep up a job and simultaneously get a degree, but she has found that even if she only spends a few minutes on each of those three projects, she makes progress and wastes less time.

Rather than procrastinating, Caroline has started using the Pomodoro Method to make writing her papers less daunting. She'll work on her paper for 25 minutes at a time, then take a quick five-minute break, during which, she'll straighten up, meditate, or check her phone notifications. She finds that she's able to focus better and get her papers completed faster and with less stress this way, which is also helping keep her grades up for the first time in a long time.

Now that Caroline's life is more organized, she has been able to find a new part-time job that offers her evening shifts. This is helping her to have fewer days where she has to wake up early, which is overall making her feel much better and less stressed. It also means that she gets to work on time.

While Matt and Caroline have not yet reached their goals, they are much closer to them, not to mention much happier and much more relaxed. They are learning to enjoy every day for what it is, rather than always waiting for that someday to be better.

# CHAPTER 6:

## GET ISH DONE

Before you can conquer the world, and be the biggest, most badass version of yourself, you need just a *couple* more pieces to the *getting shit done* puzzle. So, here we are.

**One Thing At A Time, Bro**

With technology literally everywhere, that can do literally everything, people have somehow developed the belief that they can multitask. Some people, like myself, have deluded ourselves for years, bragging about how much we thought we could get done, while simultaneously getting other things done. *Oh, yeah, I can talk on the phone, while negotiating a contract, while cooking dinner, while taking a shower, while re-planting my garden, while watching TV, while driving a go-cart. I get so much done!* I'm sorry to tell you this, but the idea that multitasking is more productive is shit. This is not just my opinion either. I've got science on my side, and there have been numerous studies on the subject.

When we believe we are multitasking, what we are actually doing is task switching, as the human brain is just not good at simultaneously concentrating on more than one item at a time. This can especially be shown when two tasks require the same area of the brain to operate. Try imagining writing a work email to your boss and talking on the phone with your grandmother simultaneously. I promise you, you'll end up writing to your boss that you want her to bake more contracts and telling your grandmother you love to sign her cookies, leaving both your boss and your grandmother utterly confused. You'll just end up getting your messages completely scrambled until you are no longer sure what you're supposed to be writing and what you're supposed to be saying and to whom. This struggle the brain undergoes in this process to make sense of things can actually be seen on brain scans in scientific studies.

Studies actually show that when we are doing what we think is "multitasking," we can decrease our productivity by up to forty freaking percent! That is quite a bit, yet many people still task switch regularly. Why? According to Professor Joyce Wang at Ohio

State University, it is because it feels emotionally satisfying, and many people believe they can get more done even if it isn't the case.

Not only can frequent task switching greatly reduce productivity, but it is also mentally taxing. The brain is constantly having to switch what information it needs to perform a task, which results in a decrease in performance that you would otherwise not experience.

Another study, this one from the University of Sussex, found that frequent task switching can even damage the brain, causing you to have lower gray matter density in the brain. This is extremely important, especially because the area of the brain it targets is the same area of the brain that controls cognitive function, emotional control, and empathy. And….yeah, we kind of need those. Making our brains go through frequent task switching also increases stress levels and can cause short-term memory loss.

A study conducted at the Institute of Psychiatry at the University of London revealed that when you multitask with electronic media, you can even cause a decrease in your IQ to a greater degree than losing a night's sleep or smoking marijuana. If that wasn't bad enough, you also lose the ability to remember much of what you learned while task switching.

Think of supposed multitasking or task switching like spending money. Each time you task switch, you are having to spend a coin, which might not be a problem if you are only task switching once an hour. But, if you are trying to "multitask" and end up task switching repeatedly and frequently in a short span of time, then you will constantly be spending money. This money costs you time, mental energy, memory, and more. You simply don't have the budget to afford it.

If you have many tasks to do and not enough time to do them, the most productive way to get through it is simply one task at a time. Because, if you are multitasking, you are spending more time on doing tasks and switching gears between tasks, when you aren't even able to accomplish them as well as you are when you are focusing on a single task.

## Permission To Be Pathetic

There are times we just can't get as much done as we wish we could. Even having a six-item to-do list, such as with the Ivy Lee method, is too much for us. I definitely know it. I've been there on numerous occasions. Sometimes it seems like everybody wants to get admitted to the hospital, have their dog die, have an existential crisis, and get stranded on the side of the road on the same day that I'm scrambling around trying to calm myself down enough to get my own stuff done. Sometimes, I just don't have time for everything.

When life is just too much, make a "pathetic" to-do list. For this list, just write two things that need to get done today. If you're feeling especially pathetic that day, hell, pick one. As long as it's the most important item you need to do, then at least you will have knocked out your most important task that will move you closer to your goals.

REESE OWEN

# CHAPTER 7:

## BADASS BLOCKERS

Can you be a bit of an ass? Do you not know how to reach your goals? Are you unsure how to set goals in the first place? Don't worry, sweetie, I've got you covered. In this chapter, we'll discuss a few other things that might be getting in the way of your success.

### Badass, Or Just An Ass?

Have you ever given much thought to who you want to be? I don't mean professionally, but generally speaking. The attributes you aspire to have, the characteristics that distinguish you from that person next to you. Who do you want to be as a whole? One of the aspects that can define your success, both in life and business, is how you present yourself. Now, this doesn't mean that terrible people are unable to become successful. The occasional douchebag does seem to slip under the radar and find some apparent success as a politician or a celebrity, but such success is often short-lived and accompanied with…well, nothing, and no one. People don't want to interact with people who are unkind, untrustworthy, and who waste their time. Nobody wants friends or business associates like this.

If you truly want to thrive in life, school, or the workplace, you need to examine yourself and consider what ways you can improve as a person. I promise you, if you can become a more kind and trustworthy person, then more people will want to be around you, to do business with you or to help you out.

If you have made it through this book that means you see that there are things you want to improve in yourself. One of the best things that you can do for yourself, other than actually implementing the advice in this book, is to examine what aspects of yourself might be getting in your own way. Every badass and badass in training has areas where they can improve.

Look deeper than your issues with procrastination, willpower, and focus for a moment. Grab a journal. Write down the things that are *really* holding you back. Sure, you procrastinate, but why do you procrastinate? Is it just because you're not organized? Or is it partially because you don't believe you can actually achieve the things you want to accomplish? Or that you don't feel that you deserve to achieve the things you want to accomplish? What limiting beliefs do you have? What non-favorable character traits do you possess? How can you be a better person? Take an inventory. Once you see everything on paper, you'll know where you need to take steps to improve, and if you do, I can guarantee that you'll start to see positive changes in your life.

## Smashing The Shit Out Of Your Goals

Have you seriously considered your goals? I don't mean simply saying "I want to own my own business" or "I want to get a degree." In order to live a purposeful life, you need to set clear-cut goals with benchmarks and timelines, so that you know where you are at in reaching said goals. You are already taking steps to reach your goals by reading this book (go, you!), but now, you need to make sure that you have an action plan on which to apply these productivity tips.

Make your goals clear, and in alignment with the things in your life that are your highest priority. If family is your highest priority, you may not want to set a goal of getting that job that pays great, but requires 80 hour work weeks with no vacation days. And be wary of having too many major life goals. You want to make sure that you're not splitting your time too much, or wearing yourself too thin to be able to have the time and energy to pursue your biggest and most important goals. I'm a person who can easily get distracted by hobbies. I'm just passionate by nature. So when I went to my first flag football meetup, and four months later, ended up starting my own team, designing uniforms, and coaching on the weekends, I had to assess the significance of what I was spending my time on. If it's taking away from my big life goals, it has to take a backseat. Participating in flag football is still something that I do because I love it, but I no longer allow it to take up my entire life.

## Be Smart About It

Perhaps you've heard of the S.M.A.R.T. goalsetting system. This acronym means that the goals you choose for yourself should be specific, measurable, attainable, relevant, and time-bound.

The goal should be specific, otherwise, you will lack sufficient direction and it will be hard to attain. Because, if you aren't even fully aware of what you want to attain, then how are you going to aim for it? Rather than having a goal of working in the food industry, have a more specific one such as wanting to own a restaurant or be head chef of a 5-star restaurant.

Make sure you can measure your success. This can look different, depending on the goal, but one instance would be if you want a specific income or specific amount in savings, you can plainly see how you have progressed over time by setting a figure as a goal in the beginning, and then monitoring and tracking your progression towards that figure. If you want to lose weight, set exactly how many pounds you want to lose, and each week or month, you can measure and track how much closer you're getting to your goal.

Be sure that your goals are attainable. You should be stretching yourself, so it shouldn't be too easy. And some people may not believe in your dream, and that is okay. That doesn't mean you should give up. Many people have attained their dreams when it seemed impossible. But, if you have a goal of being the first teenager to win an Olympic gold medal for swimming freestyle, and you're already 24, and can't swim…that one's probably not going to happen for you. Sorry.

Be sure that your goals are relevant to where you want to be in the long-term. If your goal is to go to law school, but you want to be a chef, you may want to rethink that one.

Set time limits on your goals. If you don't meet your deadline in time, it does not mean you have to give up. But, having a time limit gives us a specific time period to work towards and a sense of urgency that motivates us to take action. If someone says they want to learn a new language "someday," someday will probably never come. But, if someone says they want to be fluent in Spanish by the end of the year in time for their trip they have booked to Madrid, then they are much more likely to attain it.

Once you have set these goals, put them in writing, preferably some place you can see them regularly, and make an action plan with the steps needed to get you to seeing these goals come to fruition. These action steps will become the basis for your priority tasks that you'll put on your to do lists every night. And the most important step here is to remember to take action. Without action, nothing happens.

# CONCLUSION

Procrastination may have gotten the best of you. Maybe you've struggled with willpower. Maybe you were so overwhelmed that you didn't know where to start in getting your life in the direction you wanted it to go. Perhaps you haven't known a good goal setting system. Well, now, you have the tools you need to address all of those issues, and the fact that you sought them out and had a desire for self-improvement is already an accomplishment. Many people simply go about their mundane lives, meanwhile, life passes them by. With the tools you have learned in this book, you have everything you need to make your dreams a reality and be a more productive and effective human.

Now, let's check back in with Matt and Caroline a year later and see if this book has been working for them.

Matt is sitting as his desk in his workplace. But instead of his desk being covered in paper, it's now covered in flour. Rather than just dreaming of "someday" starting his own business, with the help of Matt's new frugal budget, he was able to quit his job, and start his cake pop business, that he has been running out of his home. Finally, after a year of hard work, creating and pursuing clear and attainable goals, asserting willpower, and ending procrastination, he's been able to start to live the life of his dreams.

He's off to a good start, having already provided his cake pop services to many local weddings and events. He's now in talks with a local coffee shop chain to get his cake pops mass produced and distributed there. Now that Matt is no longer working under his douchebag boss previous employment, he has much less stress, is able to when he wants to work, and best of all is able to spend much more time with his family.

Caroline has also managed to beat procrastination's ass, learn to strengthen her willpower, and become more organized. With the help of her new evening job schedule, and afternoon naps to recharge her night owl brain, she was able to increase her GPA in college, making her a more attractive employee candidate for future employers. She was even able to add on a couple of extra shifts at work once she had adjusted to her new organized lifestyle, and has saved up enough extra money to make a down-payment on a new car and catch up on her bills. Now that she doesn't live in total filth and squalor, her and her roommates are now besties, and one of her roommates hooked her up with a job at her mom's company that pays double what she was making and will lead to a fulltime job offer after graduation. Caroline now has a great head start on her peers, and has mastered skills that will help her conquer whatever comes her way.

While Matt and Caroline might be fictional (I'm sorry, did I just ruin it?), they represent real people with real struggles. If you picked up this book, they probably represent you and your struggles. But Matt and Caroline didn't just throw their hands up in the air, and say "Oh, well, I've always been this way," or "Life's too hard," or "It's too hard to change." They took control, took action, and made decisions that ultimately led them to better lives that leave them more fulfilled, more happy, and less *this sucks, I want to kill someone*. In the beginning of this book, we pitied Matt and Caroline. But now, I can proudly say, I want to be like Matt and Caroline when I grow up. Just like them, I want to grab life by the horns and just do the damn thing.

If you enjoyed this book in any way, please leave a review, letting us know why you loved this book. And be sure to be on the lookout for other books and audiobooks by Reese Owen.

Like what you just read?
Sad it's over?
Turn that frown upside down
and listen to the audiobook
(~~usually $14.95~~)
for **FREE**.

Search for my name
"Reese Owen" on Audible.

---

Audible member? Use a credit.
New to Audible? Get this audiobook **free**
with your free trial.

# ALL BOOKS BY REESE OWEN

Check out my other ebooks, paperback books, and audiobooks:

### B*tch Don't Kill My Vibe
How To Stop Worrying, End Negative Thinking,
Cultivate Positive Thoughts,
And Start Living Your Best Life

### Just Do The Damn Thing
How To Sit Your @ss Down Long Enough To
Exert Willpower, Develop Self Discipline,
Stop Procrastinating, Increase Productivity,
And Get Sh!t Done

### Make Your Brain Your B*tch
Mental Toughness Secrets To Rewire Your Mindset
To Be Resilient And Relentless, Have Self Confidence
In Everything You Do,
And Become The Badass You Truly Are

www.ingramcontent.com/pod-product-compliance
Lightning Source LLC
Chambersburg PA
CBHW052057110526
44591CB00013B/2252